URBAN SURPRISES:

A GUIDE TO PUBLIC ART IN LOS ANGELES

URBAN SURPRISES:
A GUIDE TO PUBLIC ART IN LOS ANGELES

EDITED BY **GLORIA GERACE**
PHOTOGRAPHS BY **DENNIS KEELEY**
INTRODUCTION BY **MARGIE J. REESE**

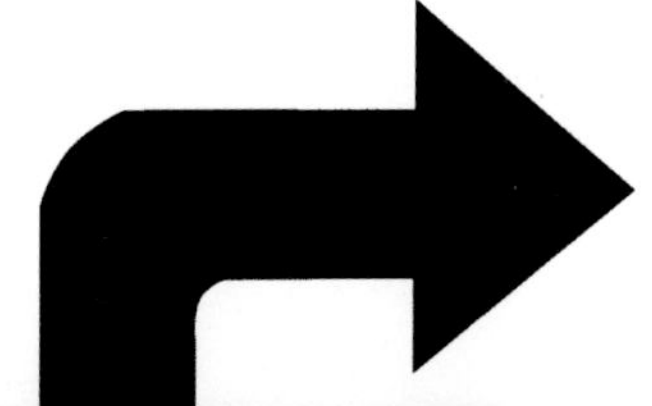

Published in the United States of America 2002
Design by Fuse Design
Printed by Navigator Press, Monrovia, California

This book was published under the auspices of the City of Los Angeles Cultural Affairs Department.
Margie J. Reeves, General Manager
Felicia Filer, Director Public Art Division

Cover Image: Lincoln Heights Library
Library of Congress Catalog Card Number: 2002103805
ISBN 1-890449-14-8

URBAN SURPRISES:

A GUIDE TO PUBLIC ART IN LOS ANGELES

TABLE OF CONTENTS

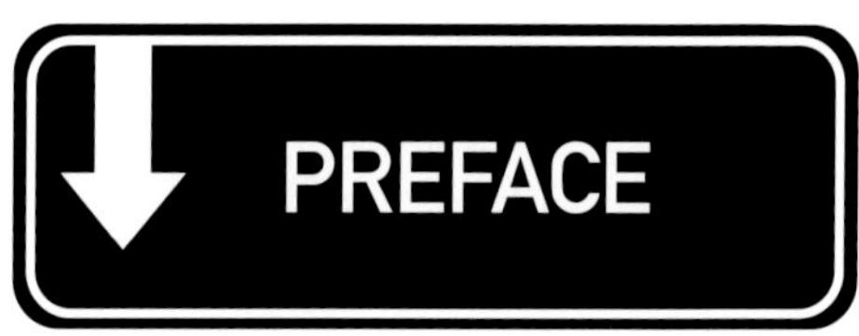

The concept of this book seemed simple enough at the beginning: a documentation of Los Angeles' public arts programs to provide a guide to works of art throughout the city. I soon discovered how vast the undertaking would be. Los Angeles, boasting one of the most productive and diverse public art programs in the nation, has hundreds and hundreds of works of art—some permanent, others temporary. Additionally, art in public places is often mislabeled as public art, causing confusion about intent and distorting the appreciation of what actually constitutes public art. This book, then, became a document of discovery—the discovery of hundreds of works of art, and the city and its people who produced them—a real urban surprise.

While this book was created through the generous sponsorship of the Cultural Affairs Department, initially the idea was to include every work of art produced through all public art programs. Since Los Angeles has numerous public art programs, one of the first, and most difficult, tasks was how to focus this book from an editorial and a reader's point of view. In the end, we decided to limit the scope to works of art produced under the aegis of three programs: the City of Los Angeles Cultural Affairs Department's Public Art Programs, the Community Redevelopment Agency's Downtown Art in Public Places, and Los Angeles County's Metropolitan Transit Authority's Metro Art Department. Each of these three programs is tied to new construction; each program focuses on a slightly different direction; and, each program is active and prolific, jointly producing the over three hundred and forty works of art featured in this book.

Working on this book developed into an amazing adventure that was both a physical journey through Los Angeles and a metaphysical journey of discovering Los Angeles. With Dennis Keeley, the talented and generous artist whose photographs grace these pages, I traveled through a city that defies definition and boundaries. While we journeyed to the communities of San Pedro, Chatsworth, Boyle Heights, Venice, South Central, Northridge, Koreatown, downtown, and Echo Park, we encountered the reality of a city unimaginable in complexity, scope, and diversity.

Our encounters with the communities where these works of art reside and the people who live and work among them, reinforced our notions of Los Angeles as a city of the most unexpected moments. At a Northridge car dealership, the sales staff proudly showed us their painting by Paul Tzanetopoulos and shared their interpretations of the painting, which they discuss when business is slow. At the Newton Police Station, the officers were insistent that we see all of the pieces made for their station by Richard Turner, not only the first one in the lobby. In the frantic export/import district of downtown, we traveled through blocks of warehouses to arrive at a building entry that is graced by an exquisite mosaic with Islamic and Hindu motifs by Barbara Field. At the Los Angeles Chamber of Commerce headquarters, the staff told us that we needed to come back at various times of day to really appreciate the Simon Toparovsky water sculpture in different daylight conditions.

Our visits to the branch libraries of the Los Angeles Public Library were especially rewarding. These buildings resonate with the history of the city. We relished the fact that nestled in every corner of this vast city, lies one of these gems; and we looked forward to each mesmerizing visit. And, we learned that the librarians, who serve these places, are not only stewards of books, but cultural ambassadors, community leaders, homework helpers, and neighborhood friends.

Documenting the works of art presented a challenge. Public art is alive and in flux: new projects constantly emerge; existing projects are often transformed through the natural evolution of a community; buildings change ownership and/or function; and occasionally, sites are demolished altogether. We decided that this book would include only those projects that could be documented and were completed by December 2001. Our hope was that interest in the public art of Los Angeles would generate a curiosity on the part of the reader to discover many works of urban art not included in this book.

In 1992, I had the opportunity to work with an exceptional group of historians, artists, sociologists, and activists, who as research associates assembled by Harold M. Williams, then President of the J. Paul Getty Trust, worked on a series of projects related to Los Angeles. On a daily basis, one of them would visit me, announcing that they had "something amazing that we needed to know." Indeed, they had; and through them, I learned to think about this city in a new way. I learned that it is all there, I just needed to find it. This book, dedicated to that remarkable group, follows their charge; the public art of Los Angeles is amazing and you need to know about it. – **GLORIA GERACE**

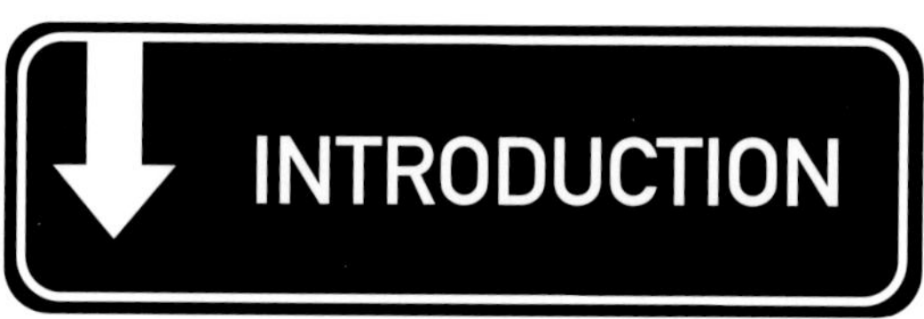

Los Angeles—just take a look at our city!

This publication—***A Guide to Public Art in Los Angeles***—should serve as your road map to seeing the traditions, cultural values and imagination of numerous artists whose public artworks create, define and reflect Los Angeles. From the earliest sculptures created in Little Tokyo to the spectrum of works found at the subway stations to the contemporary murals that describe culturally distinct neighborhoods, this guide welcomes you to take a look at our city.

Public art shapes the look of a city and gives identity to a place. This guide illustrates the significant role that artists have had in shaping the look of Los Angeles. Artists bring a refreshing sensibility to the planning process: an unexpected artistic twist in solving a problem, an ability to nurture new insights, an understanding of the connections between people and places and an enthusiasm to foster civic pride. Without these artists' vision, ingenuity and creative expression, Los Angeles would not be what we see and experience today.

Diversity is an overused word by some, but when describing Los Angeles' public art, it is the only word that describes these projects, from the neighborhoods where they are found to the stories each artwork tells about people, places and practices. Our city's public art is a mirror of our city's distinct neighborhoods. It can show who used to live there and who lives there now. Like many cities in the United States, Los Angeles' community demographics are constantly changing as people move in and out of neighborhoods. Public art often remains a constant, thereby serving as a cultural legacy of those earlier communities. As new people move into a community, the existing public art provides a sense of place and history. It represents a physical documentation of the people who were there before and reveals their values, traditions and customs.

The whole of the public art created in Los Angeles is an ongoing commitment by the city realized through three separate governmental agencies. The agencies which commissioned the public artworks highlighted in this guide are the City of Los Angeles Cultural Affairs Department, the Community Redevelopment Agency and Los Angeles County's Metropolitan Transit Authority. Each agency manages public art projects that fall within their respective jurisdictions. Together these three agencies are responsible for facilitating the creation of a diverse body of public artworks for Los Angeles.

No matter which agency commissioned the artworks found in this guide, the three public art programs seek to accomplish the same goal. We are all partners in the creation of engaging, meaningful and thoughtful public art for Los Angeles and hope that this guide demonstrates the individual agencies' dedication to that goal.

So, take a look at L.A. and use this guide to discover some of the most wondrous surprises of its lively, vibrant public art programs.

MARGIE J. REESE
General Manager
City of Los Angeles Cultural Affairs Department

WHAT IS PUBLIC ART?

A descriptive phrase and label used by millions, "public art" has a different meaning, especially in the art world, than commonly perceived. Often, the term is used in reference to a work of art located in a public place; however, "public art," as defined by cities throughout the United States, implies a work of art created through a public process. Moreover, in Los Angeles, the notion that it describes an over-sized sculpture plopped down in the vicinity of a building is as out of date as "making a carbon copy." It is an anomalous description of contemporary urban design, being generally associated with art as some form of decoration. Art as an object is the standard in academia and the marketplace and is the form most easily understood in a world of business. However, just as commerce has shifted to provide service, artistic endeavor in the public realm has also changed. What is at the forefront today has evolved along with architectural planning and design and provides an active infrastructure for human interaction and learning beyond the physical site.

The Cultural Affairs Department of the City of Los Angeles maintains certain assumptions about public art, including:

- Public art is both product and process.
- Public art is not intended as decoration of the urban environment.
- Public art may be different than art of the moment (what is fashionable).
- A role of the City is to foster the "laboratory" of public art.

Public art has two basic components—process and product. One need only shop from a catalog of available art if product is the most valued of these components. Similarly, it is possible to exclude the "art as therapy or social service" approach to process. In the City of Los Angeles, both process and product are given equal consideration and weight and are both used to judge a project's success. Another important measure is how funding gets to the arts, particularly to artists. A public art budget should not reflect payment on a professional level to the engineer, architect, fabricator and installer, with only a token honorarium for the artist. It is also important that funded projects develop, encourage, and support the cultural and artistic life of the City in a manner that affects the citizenry at large. For this reason, a majority of public art projects are commissioned from artists who reside in metropolitan Los Angeles. Public art is not a means of introduction for non-resident artists. Museums, galleries, and other grant programs can adequately perform that function.

When the desired project outcome is a physical work of art, collaboration between artist and project design team is the most effective scenario. Most successful artistic solutions develop a dialog with the environment from the very first concepts and sketches. In this way, the art is not distinct from the building but can use its materials, palette and vocabulary. For example, the artist can select the colors and patterns of the terrazzo floor on the ground level, or a pattern on or in the elevators. Sometimes the contributions of architect and artist are indistinguishable, but whatever is done, the artist's contribution will have an effect on the architecture and its users. Ideally, the artist's influences are felt in the design process as much as, if not more so, than in the product.

The artist works with the community—workers, visitors, users, clients, and those living in the area—to develop the narrative aspect of the artistic intervention. This may involve history, issues of contemporary concern, or may simply enlarge the purpose of the architecture. An artist is the 'shaman' in this interaction: channeling, interpreting, and distilling ideas to create a community dialog and a work of art.

The artist as shaman differs from the traditional role of the contemporary artist as a lone figure struggling in the studio, seeking the creative muse. By contrast, an artist practicing in the public realm has a dialog with people, which influences and affects the final work. Conversely, that interchange affects the people who interact with the artist. It is not too surprising that this is how a community may assign value, and consequently assume custodial care, for a piece of art. It represents much more than the sum of its visual parts.

Public art needs to accommodate the architectural, social, and cultural circumstances within which it is placed. Forty years ago, it was appropriate for contemporary sculpture to move outside the limitations of a gallery or museum and augment progressive architectural design. Thirty years ago, the definition was expanded to include historic architectural renovation and community generated projects. In either scenario, the artist's role was that of contributor—and that effort was deemed relevant "for the greater good." However, a democracy depends on interaction among people. This may be translated into the artist forming a team of fabricators, installers, planners, other artists, and people from the community. Participation may take many different forms and include politicians, patrons, art cognoscenti, owners, and inhabitants of an area. Today, public art considers the voices from these varied definitions of community. It also assumes an active role in the life of an area after construction.

While public art programs differ administratively in the private and public sectors, both focus on the community. In the public sector, the library system underwent a vigorous program of renovation and expansion. Libraries are communal gathering places, and the City recognized the opportunity to humanize and activate these spaces with art. To this end, the public art in City of Los Angeles libraries is among the most advanced in the country. Finished and future projects involve over fifty artists as contributors to new or renovated libraries. Since 1998, there has been a concerted effort toward the early integration of an artist in the project design process in order to expand the potential artistic intervention.

The private sector is required by law to contribute to the community through art through the Arts Development Fee (ADF), a fee enacted to counterbalance the lack of monies for the arts and culture. This title was not developed arbitrarily from political discussions, but is rooted in practical application. The best method for funding new art programs and artwork has been through the opportunity of new construction, which has been the most effective way to monitor population shifts and the condition of existing facilities. The term, Arts Development, was chosen as it supports all artistic expression— including any imaginable form of visual art, dance, theater, music, and education.

From 1996 to the present, the thrust of Arts Development Fee activities has been toward the development of art programs as opposed to art installations. Over $3,000,000 has been directed toward creative and innovative plans that bring dance, theater, music, film, poetry, and the visual arts directly to the communities where specific developments have been built. These include: the establishment of endowments supporting free musical programs; monies to small budget organizations for performance and educational outreach; bringing working artists into elementary and high schools for projects and classes; awards to arts organizations for storage, office space or advertising; and artist designed beautification of existing public schools facilities.

Administratively, there is an ongoing question of how to simultaneously accommodate the cultural needs of the City, support individual artistic vision, and tailor the solution for any project to specific circumstances. There is an imperative to determine community needs, to be comfortably conversant with all parties, and to maximize the project's effectiveness. An administrator must be a good negotiator and grapple with the demands of the present and maintain an overall vision. One must educate, have an ability to assess a situation, think creatively, and adapt to changing circumstances. The ultimate role of the administrator is to be a guerrilla advocate for the arts, suggesting and supporting new ideas. In some ways, this implies trust in the process rather than the product.

It is easier to give mature artists the tools to navigate the process than to teach artists how to deal with the process maturely. When artists are commissioned to create something physical for a site, the learning curve involves being part of a team and becoming familiar with the give and take of collaboration. It may also involve a presentation of ideas, and negotiation with the public. There are also practical considerations such as wear and tear of public exposure, maintenance, and long-term relevance. Architecture is usually approached with an attitude of permanence; however, the reality is that much construction is planned with a discrete life span. Should the art made for it also have an anticipated obsolescence? This might be another way of measuring the life of public art. Public art is a laboratory and should not be any more permanent than the buildings where it happens to occur. Artists should adapt to using that strategy as a basis for their creative solutions.

It is unreasonable to think that all the art created for display in galleries and museums merits eternal life. It is also unreasonable to imagine that all public art should exist indefinitely. Artists—and administrators—need to think of it as a form of exploration, to proceed from what is known and to test the unknown.

The process of public art—and the individuals administering it—must constantly change. Attitudes can be introduced as an educational component of the process and, in fact, must always be a part of public art. The kind of questions that should be posed are: "What is already offered in the community?" "What opportunities exist for artists in the community?" and "What artistic efforts will benefit the community, either short or long term?" Education must constantly be applied to all parts of the equation—from funding to builder to user. The only limits are those of human imagination. – **ROELLA HSIEH LOUIE**

BUILDING COMMUNITY

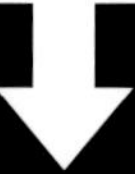

> A SOCIETY THAT VALUES ART IS NOT LIKELY TO MISTAKE SAMENESS FOR EQUALITY, A DISTINCTION FUNDAMENTAL TO THE VITAL COMBINATION OF SOCIAL JUSTICE AND CULTURAL PLURALISM.
>
> – JEROLD M. STARR, CULTURAL POLITICS: RADICAL MOVEMENT IN MODERN HISTORY

Residents and visitors experience Los Angeles, primarily, by car. Driving through the city, one glimpses various works of art in public spaces—sculptures, fountains, murals, mosaics, fences, stained-glass windows, benches, and more. Some pieces are in open areas, easily viewed; others are beyond view, tucked inside the built environment. Wherever it resides, the public art of Los Angeles is interesting, provocative, and, at times, transcendent. Each project, in some way, offers a respite from the workday routine and provides a sense of place, a point of beauty, or a means of individual growth and development. More importantly, in a city as diverse and vast as Los Angeles, public art builds community—from the very germ of its inception, to the physical realization of an artist's vision, to the enjoyment of the finished work of art.

It is likely that Los Angeles residents or visitors have passed one or more of the works of art featured in this book and have wondered: "Why is it there? How does art materialize in public places?" Cities initiated public art programs in the 1960s when urban flight sparked the recognition of aging city centers as well as the effort to rehabilitate them. Public art was seen as a way to ameliorate the physical environment and alleviate the growing alienation of residents and their communities. Planners elevated the role of public spaces, allowing art to reflect surrounding communities, and thus created places of pride and visual focus. For those living or working in a city center, public art defined new (or enriched existing) communal space. Over the ensuing years, artists, sponsors, and administrators of public art programs have shifted from the monumental–the statue in the plaza–to a strategy in which aesthetic, functional, and educational purposes coexist and collectively create community.

Public art in Los Angeles is realized in many ways and is best understood within the context and intent unique to each piece. Diversity is Los Angeles' greatest strength, its greatest challenge, and its greatest promise. As public art evolves amid an increasingly diverse population, it can become an important vehicle for beginning a dialog and making art a viable part of public life.

Whatever form Percent for Art takes, "public art" is a dynamic mediation between the private and the public; the individual and the group; and most importantly, it is a catalyst for community development. Public art is not only about a work of art; it is also about the process. There are times when the outcome may be disappointing, but the process itself—stimulating community interest and participation, helping a community to crystallize a vision of itself and communicating that vision to the city at large—may have generated very successful results. Public art becomes meaningful if it embodies a shared cultural perspective, which is gained by exploring broad and narrow perspectives of individuals and communities.

Every public art project involves a process of negotiation and discovery, education and reward. The commissioning process is complex and encourages different groups through varying degrees of access and participation to work toward the final outcome. The role of staff in the Public Art Program is to educate and facilitate. Each party involved in the process of creating public art presents its own challenges. Private developers, for instance, may not focus on their role in the community because, after all, they are developing private spaces. However, developers may play an important public role and have many options for participation in the Public Art Program than they initially envision. For example, one developer built warehouses in the garment district where a site-specific artwork was not as beneficial as his choice to give the neighboring inner city junior high school $18,000 worth of new musical instruments.

Communities are organic—they change. Each must consider whether or not the art they select will contribute to future inhabitants. Is it going to provide some kind of education and inspiration for the future? Is it going to convey the essence and importance of community space? How does it reflect the community?

The artists who create works of public art must incorporate the process into their work in an intense way. They must interact with communities, a number of city departments, a specific context, and the political process. For those artists who persevere–from putting forth their proposal to the unveiling of the completed project–the rewards of seeing their work as part of the cityscape are incalculable.

The passerby, the neighbor, the art enthusiast, or the city dweller, are those for whom public art and the attendant process are intended. In the Department's role as educators and facilitators, those who are part of the Public Art Program hope that this book will enlighten and encourage everyone to experience the public art in Los Angeles, on the city's streets and in its buildings. Los Angeles is surprisingly rich in community spirit and creativity. – **MARK JOHNSTONE**

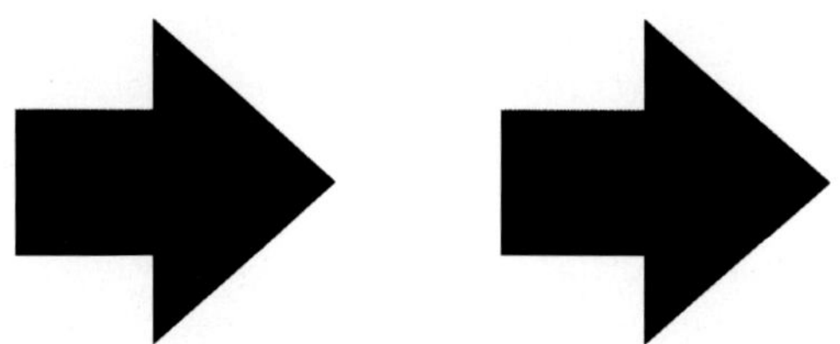

CITY OF LOS ANGELES CULTURAL AFFAIRS DEPARTMENT PUBLIC ART PROGRAMS

There are two "Percent for Art" programs mandated by ordinance in the City of Los Angeles—the Arts Development Fee and the Public Works Improvements Arts Program. The Arts Development Fee administered by the Cultural Affairs Department, is applied to all non-residential construction with a building valuation of over $500,000. In that program the developer must submit a plan (artist, art concept) to the Cultural Affairs Department for approval before issuance of the building permit. The expenditure is either an assessment per square foot, based on the planned use, or one percent of the building valuation that appears on the building permit (which is usually different from actual construction costs)—whichever is lower. The purpose of the Public Works Improvements Arts Program is to include art in all capital improvement projects undertaken by the City. That program stipulates an amount equal to one percent of the construction value of the building shall be allocated by the City as part of its overall project budget.

The goal of both programs is to provide innovation and collaboration, and to remove any barriers that may discourage artists and the community from participating in public art programs. Seeking to encourage wide participation by artists, when the City anticipates the need for art in an upcoming PWIAP project, a call for artists is mailed to the public art division database as well as posted to a web page. A selection panel is convened to review all submissions and select five finalists to prepare and

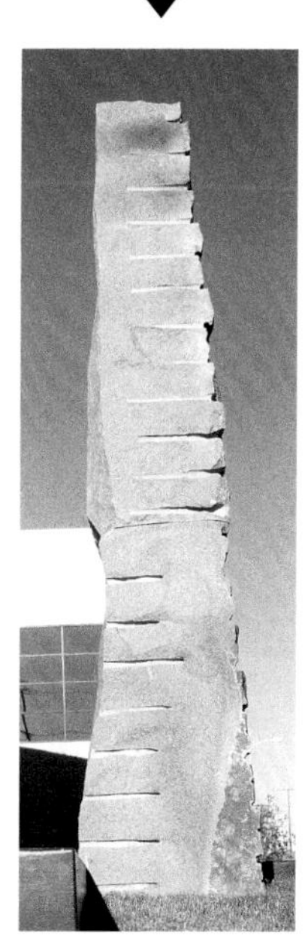

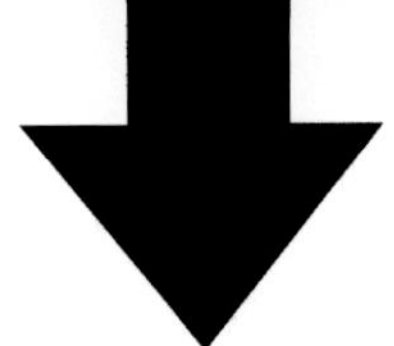

present a proposal for which the artists are compensated. Each finalist makes a presentation to the selection panel, which then awards the commission to one artist/team. Typically, the artist will present the artwork proposal to the community before finalizing the concept, soliciting community input and allowing for possible revisions to the concept. The artist must then present the proposal to a series of City committees, commissions, and possibly a client department.

In Public Works projects, a community meeting allows for interaction between artist, local community groups, users of the facilities and other interested parties. The community plays an important future role in the process, for they will also be the users and caretakers of the work. Several assumptions are inherent in the process, including the need for education about the art, and budgets allocated for maintenance or conservation. – **FELICIA FILER**

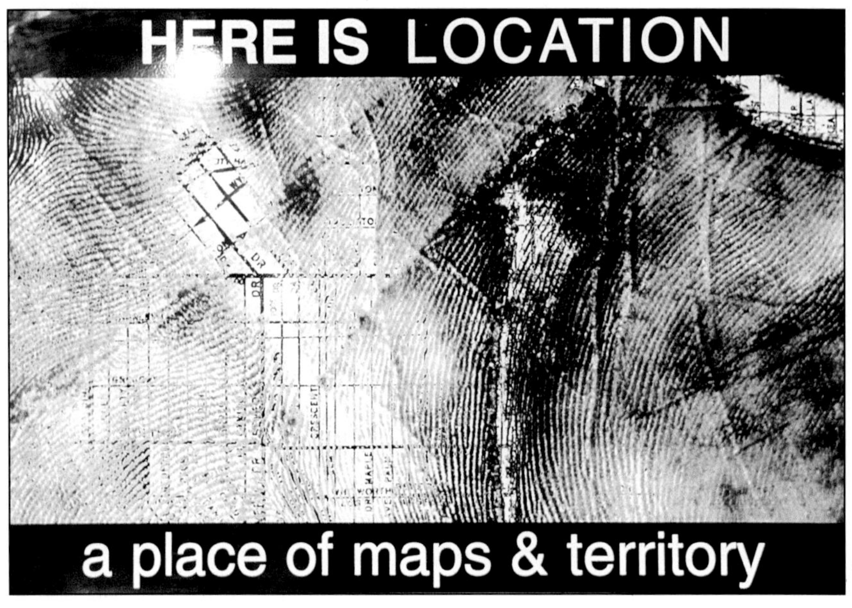

71] ROBERTSON PARKING STRUCTURE

CAD PUBLIC ART

1] SITE **Motion Picture Association of America** / ADDRESS **15503 Ventura Boulevard, Encino, 91436** / ARTIST **Margaret Nielsen** / TITLE/DESC.**Hollywood Highlights; glass mosaic inlay** / LOCATION **Exterior (columns)** / DATE **1994**

Artist Margaret Nielsen designed twenty-one, mosaic inlay panels of Venetian glass, using images from familiar Hollywood motion pictures. The panels are installed on columns surrounding the front of the building plaza.

2] SITE **Temple Valley Beth Shalom** / ADDRESS **15739 Ventura Boulevard, Encino, 91436** / ARTIST **David & Michelle Plachte-Zuieback** / TITLE/DESC **Untitled; stained glass windows** / LOCATION **Exterior/Interior** / DATE **1991**

The artists designed and fabricated the stained glass windows in the Temple's main entrance. The windows incorporate letters from the Hebrew alphabet, geometric designs, and traditional Jewish iconography.

3] SITE **Encino Marketplace** / ADDRESS **16325 Ventura Boulevard, Encino, 91436** / ARTIST **Jose Antonio Aguirre** / TITLE/DESC **1] La Dama de Rojo; tile mosaic 2] The Valley Spirit; fountain** / LOCATION **Exterior** / DATE **1994**

Jose Antonio Aguirre created a mural and fountain in the traditional technique of Byzantine, Venetian glass mosaic and glass mirror mosaic. The mural was inspired by the history of the San Fernando Valley, from its beginnings as a desert to its present urban form.

4] SITE **South West Aviation** / ADDRESS **7150 Hayvenhurst Avenue, Van Nuys, 91406** / ARTIST **Jim Jenkins** / TITLE **Untitled; sculpture** / LOCATION Exterior / DATE **1996**

Jenkins' monument to aviation stands over ten feet tall at the intersection of Sherman Way and Hayvenhurst Avenue. The aircraft wing-shaped sculpture was included in South West Aviation's new aircraft hangar and administrative buildings at Van Nuys Airport.

5] SITE **Food for Less/Vest Associates** / ADDRESS **16500-16530 Sherman Way, Van Nuys, 91406** / ARTIST **Rod Baer** / TITLE/DESC. **Flying on Neon Thermals; neon sculpture** / LOCATION **Exterior** / DATE **1994**

Artist Rod Baer designed a large-scale "paper airplane" made from neon and aluminum with a painted surface. This work, which has a sign component, is consistent with the nearby Van Nuys Airport.

6] SITE **Petersen Aviation** / ADDRESS **7155 Valjean Avenue, Van Nuys, 91406** / ARTIST **Douglas Van Howd** / TITLE/DESC. **Untitled; bronze sculpture** / LOCATION **Exterior** / DATE **1993**

Petersen Aviation commissioned the artist to create a sculpture for the site. Van Howd's eagle in flight has a wingspan of approximately sixteen feet and appears to soar effortlessly. The sculpture rests on a stainless steel base, which bears the Petersen logo in bronze.

7] SITE **Beechcraft West** / LOCATION **7240 Hayvenhurst Avenue, Van Nuys, 91406** / ARTIST **Michael Hayden** / TITLE/DESC. **Transrotation; sculpture** / LOCATION **Interior** / DATE **1994**

This sculptural relief, named "Transrotation," is located behind the customer service counter area in the building's foyer. The sculpture consists of a series of holographic semi-circles, which incorporate fiber optic technology, against a mirrored surface to create the illusion of a sphere "rotating" in space.

8] SITE **The Lewis Company** / ADDRESS **15853 Strathern Street, Van Nuys, 91406** / ARTIST **Woods Davy** / TITLE **Untitled; sculpture** / LOCATION **Exterior** / DATE **1998**

The artist created a sculpture for each of the building entrances in the four-building complex. The rough-hewn, gray stone sculptures are placed at various angles and have metal plinths for bases.

9] SITE **Anheuser-Busch** / ADDRESS **16135 Roscoe Boulevard, North Hills, 91343** / ARTIST **Susan Narduli, Liz Larner** / TITLE **Untitled; brushed aluminum and neon sculpture** / LOCATION **Exterior** / DATE **1993**

Narduli and Larner combined motifs of plants used in the brewing process with birds in flight to create a design for the building façade. An eagle was incorporated to refer to the corporate logo. The pieces are cut from brushed aluminum, which has a reflective surface that is sensitive to atmospheric conditions and artificial or natural light. Red and white neon provide the source of back lighting for the piece.

10] SITE **Mid-Valley Regional Branch Library** / ADDRESS **16244 Nordoff Boulevard, North Hills, 91343** / ARTIST **John Wehrle** / TITLE/DESC **Scribes; mural** / LOCATION **Interior** / DATE **1995**

The artist combined painted figures and text to create a whimsical piece that shows the written word flowing through the library. The mural's scribes are rendered monochromatically in the manner of relief carving, and appear to have the powers of levitation as they install various quotes about books, reading, and language. The central atrium of the library is painted to mimic sky and clouds, as is the wall in the young readers' section. Here, the scribes are children spelling out the word, "DREAM."

11] SITE **J & B Development** / ADDRESS **9846 White Oak Avenue, Northridge, 91325** / ARTIST **Debbie Montrose** / TITLE/DESC **All Tiled Up; mural, tile mosaic** / LOCATION **Exterior** / DATE **1992**

Architect Peter Magaro worked closely with artist Debbie Montrose and the owner to create a project consistent with the building's contemporary design. The abstract tile mosaic, with its dynamic, free-flowing expression of color and movement, is part of the building structure.

12] SITE **Granada Hills Community Center** / ADDRESS **16730 Chatsworth Street, Granada Hills, 91344** / ARTIST **Anthony Pardines** / TITLE/DESC **Untitled; photography collection** / LOCATION **Interior** / DATE **2000**

A series of photographic portraits of the community occupies the Center's hallways. At the entrance, three images symbolize "The Generations," youth, adults, and elders. Further along, twenty-seven portraits represent the many faces of the community. Fourteen images of objects and places that represent Granada Hills create a complete image of the community.

13] SITE **Mini-Med** / ADDRESS **18000 Devonshire Street, Canoga Park, 91304** / ARTIST **Susan Wickstrand** / TITLE/DESC **Water Feature; collection** / LOCATION **Exterior; Interior** / DATE **1996**

Susan Wickstrand created a rock and water feature for the plaza of the eastern courtyard that appears to erupt from the flat concrete. A series of purchased and commissioned artwork includes Wickstrand's "Fathers of Invention," "The Dawn of a New Day: Homage to Alfred E Mann (Court of the Patriarchs, Mt. Zion Utah)," and three pieces from Ruth Weisberg: "Family," "Chatsworth Terrain," and "Northridge Terrain." Work by William Smith, Adam Wolpert, and Darren Waterston are also included.

14] SITE **J&B Development** / ADDRESS **9836 White Oak Avenue, Northridge, 91325** / ARTIST **Kris Holliday** / TITLE/DESC **Triune; mosaic tile mural** / LOCATION **Exterior** / DATE **2001**

Under the supervision of Kim Abeles, Associate Professor in the Fine Arts department at the California State University, Northridge, students in the graduate program submitted proposals to design and develop a public art project. After a review of proposals, the developer offered the commission to artist Kris Holliday. Holliday's mosaic rose depicts three simple wave shapes that represent either smoke or water. The title, Triune, refers to three parts coming together to make a whole.

15] SITE **Sun Valley Metrolink Station** / ADDRESS **8358 San Fernando Road, Sun Valley, 91326** / ARTIST **Paul Tzanetopoulos** / TITLE/DESC **Untitled; mosaic tile** / LOCATION **Exterior** / DATE **1999**

The artist designed a decorative mosaic wall that surrounds a storm drain. The colors and patterning of the tiles refer to the water flowing through the storm drain. The MTA and City of Los Angeles Cultural Affairs Department jointly commissioned and funded this project.

16] SITE **Acapulco Restaurants, Inc.** / ADDRESS **9400 Reseda Blvd., Northridge, 91324** / ARTIST **Patti Lewis, Rosemary Garcia, Don Smith** / TITLE/DESC **Collection** / LOCATION **Interior** / DATE **1991**

Murals, sculpture, architectural elements, and pottery were commissioned for the restaurant and dispersed throughout.

17] SITE **Toyota** / ADDRESS **19550 Nordhoff Street, Northridge, 91324** / ARTIST **Paul Tzanetopoulos** / TITLE/DESC **Stirring Designs; painting** / LOCATION **Interior** / DATE **1995**

"Stirring Designs" is from a series of artwork entitled "Auto Malapropos" and consists of images of vehicles with hub caps or wheels belonging to distinctly different models. The piece, lacquer on gessoed canvas over a wood frame, is located in the main building lobby.

18] SITE **American Diversified** / ADDRESS **19500 Plummer Street, Northridge, 91324** / ARTIST **Edmond E. Shumpert** / TITLE/DESC **Neptune Fountain; bronze sculpture** / LOCATION **Exterior** / DATE **1998**

Shumpert's bronze rendition of the god Neptune sits on an extensive fountain installation, which consists of a series of jet sprays followed by water pouring from an upper tide pool through rocks.

19] SITE **Medical Park Plaza/Unihealth** / ADDRESS **18546 Roscoe Boulevard, Northridge, 91325** / ARTIST **1] Manfred Mueller 2] Sandra Rowe** / TITLE **1] Eternal Ring, Symbol of Life; neon sculpture 2] The Wellness Project; mixed media on paper** / LOCATION **Exterior/ Interior** / DATE **1995**

Mueller's exterior sculpture frames and defines the building entrance with a circular form that represents wholeness and wellness. Rowe's series of three mixed media works on paper, located in the building lobby, centers on the theme of wellness.

20] SITE **Northridge Metrolink Station, Ventura Line** / ADDRESS **8701 Wilbur Avenue, Northridge, 91324** / ARTIST **Will Nettleship** / TITLE/DESC **Untitled; architectural element** / LOCATION: **Exterior/Interior** / DATE **2000**

The artist has interpreted the theme of city and country as the condition of the commuter. Images of a distant cityscape juxtaposed with a detailed image of a citrus tree branch are stamped into the pavement at the three entrances. The images then become relief panels cast into the station walls. As the passengers move to a shaded canopy area, the images appear on glass block. The MTA and the City of Los Angeles Cultural Affairs Department jointly commissioned and funded this project.

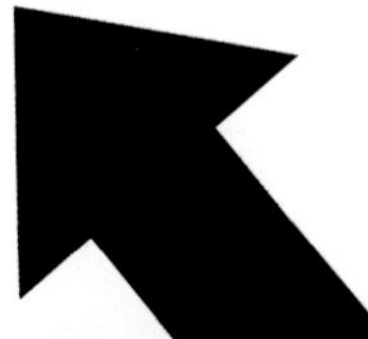

URBAN INSTALLATIONS

To mediate the hard reality of buildings like parking structures, police stations, and recycling centers, artists have attempted to bring humor, human scale, visual relief, and a sense of discovery to the urban landscape. As artist Rod Baer said in describing his work for the Robertson Parking Structure, "The inside of the parking structure is relatively straightforward and anonymous; however, the surrounding neighborhood does have a very specific character. Rather than thinking of this parking structure as empty space that could be 'anywhere,' I asked myself to begin to think of what makes this anonymous space 'here.' Discovering how we define 'here' — as a physical location and socio-historical moment within larger conceptual frameworks — became the subject and imagery of the artwork. In the end, the piece took on a more serious and poetic aspect than more mainstream public commissions, but I think it is a good thing that people will be surprised to discover such art in an unexpected place."
Many of the works of art were commissioned for public facilities that are bound by the same Percent for Art requirement as private building projects. One of the challenges for the artists is to balance the public and private nature of the buildings, as Joe Sam points out about his piece, "My goal in designing the art of the 77th Street Regional Policy Facility was to enhance the environment and to make it feel not only safe, but also warm and welcoming. At the same time, I wanted to create a space where police officers could find some reprieve from their demanding work and regenerate themselves."

The following locations are examples of art as an urban installation:

ROBERTSON PARKING STRUCTURE

VENICE CROSSROADS PARKING LOT

NEWTON POLICE STATION

77TH STREET REGIONAL POLICY FACILITY

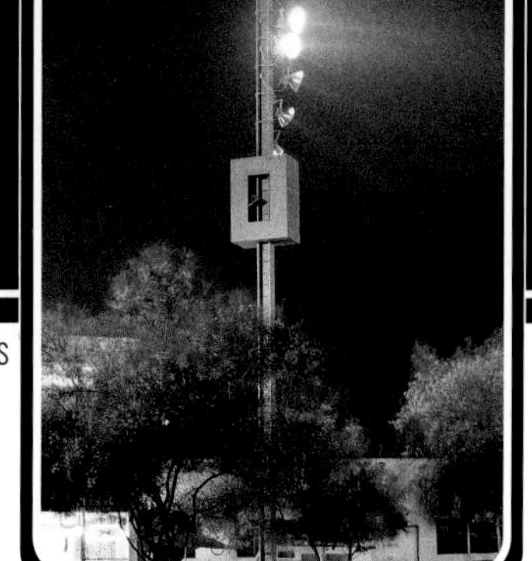

80] VENICE CROSSROADS PARKING LOT LIGHTPOLES

21] SITE **Jewish Home for the Aging** / ADDRESS **7150 Tampa Avenue, Valencia, 91355** / ARTIST **Ruth Snyder, Laurie Gross, Donna Weisner, Michele Boyer** / TITLE/DESC **Untitled; sculpture garden** / LOCATION **Exterior** / DATE **1991**

The Jewish Home for the Aging commissioned, installed and continues to maintain sculpture by various artists. The works of art, created in a variety of motifs, are located throughout the campus and are the beginning of an ongoing Sculpture Garden Program.

22] SITE **Telesis Federal Credit Union** / ADDRESS **9301 N. Winnetka Avenue, Woodland Hills, 91367** / ARTIST **Starlie Sokol-Hohne, Laddie John Dill, Richard Hall, Mark Sumner** / TITLE/DESC **Collection** / LOCATION **Interior** / DATE **1999**

Telesis Federal Credit Union commissioned eleven pieces by four artists and installed the pieces throughout their building. The works include three mixed-media pieces by Starlie Sokol-Hohne, a custom wall sculpture by Laddie John Dill, three original works on paper by Mark Sumner, and four monoprints by Richard Hall

23] SITE **Chatsworth Products** / ADDRESS **9353 N. Winnetka, Woodland Hills, 91367** / ARTIST **Susan Landau** / TITLE/DESC **Untitled; copper and stainless steel sculpture** / LOCATION **Exterior** / DATE **2000**

For Chatsworth Products, an employee owned corporation, Susan Landau created a sculpture of seven figures with a wall mounted copper canopy, and two figures installed on concrete pads. The installation was placed next to the facility's landscaped, rear entrance.

24] SITE **3 D Enterprises** / ADDRESS **19019 Ventura Boulevard, Tarzana, 91356** / ARITST **Leonora Carrington** / TITLE/DESC **Noche de Luna, Arte Marcial, and Las Esquina; paintings** / LOCATION **Interior** / DATE **1990**

3-D Enterprises acquired 3 paintings by artist Leonora Carrington. "Noche de Luna" is a mixed media work, created circa 1950 . "Arte Marcial" is a watercolor, created circa 1980. " Las Esquina" is also a watercolor, created circa 1980.

25] SITE **Tarzana Childcare Center** / ADDRESS **5655 Vanalden Avenue, Tarzana, 91356** / ARTIST **Eugenia Butler and Annie Chu** / TITLE/DESC **Untitled; Frieze panels and landscaping** / LOCATION **Exterior/interior** / DATE **2000**

A birch plywood panel frieze with brightly stained silhouettes of children runs along the walls of the Center's lobby. Outside, between the drop-off area and the main entrance, is an interactive, landscaped space that contains three curved walls of pigmented concrete leading to the entrance. Both decorative and functional, the walls act as retaining walls and some as benches.

26] SITE **Woodland Hills Country Club** / ADDRESS **21150 Dumetz Road, Woodland Hills, 91364** / ARTIST **Robert Tittle; Diana Philbrook; Mark King** / TITLE/DESC **Untitled; various** / LOCATION **Interior** / DATE **1992**

Woodland Hills Country Club commissioned several projects and offered exhibition space for the Art League of Los Angeles. Architect Robert Tittle designed a chandelier to provide a focal point for the lobby. Diana Philbrook painted a series of historical montages to celebrate the history of the Club, and Mark King created a series of colorful serigraphs to accent the Club's walls.

27] SITE **Tishman Warner Center** / ADDRESS **21271 Burbank Boulevard, Woodland Hills, 91367** / ARTIST **May Sun** / TITLE/DESC **Art Walls; architectural elements** / LOCATION **Interior** / DATE **2000**

"Art Walls," designed by May Sun, is located in the building's main lobby. The work, made from Jerusalem stone with varying textures, is strategically arranged to complement the nature and placement of the individual art pieces. The pieces consist of approximately 33 brass inlays and 12 etched copper alloy panels, which reflect the rich history of the west San Fernando Valley.

28] SITE **Rick Gelb** / ADDRESS **22025 Ventura Boulevard, Woodland Hills, 91364** / ARTIST **Alvin T. Dickens and Dick Starkweather** / TITLE/DESC **Untitled; sculpture** / LOCATION **Exterior** / DATE **1991**

Rick Gelb commissioned artists Alvin T. Dickens and Dick Starkweather to create a glass block wall with colored lights that rotate on set intervals and change the colors of the glass. The wall is located on the exterior of the elevator tower at the front of the building.

29] SITE **Platt Branch Library** / ADDRESS **23650 Victory Boulevard, Woodland Hills, 91367** / ARTIST **Gale McCall** / TITLE/DESC **Sculpture: tracery metal murals** / LOCATION **Interior** / DATE **1995**

A series of tracery filigree metal work is attached beneath four of the major beams spanning the library's central room. The sculpture elements are transparent murals, which are legible from either side. The images include familiar symbols, patterns, and motifs referring to reading and the community's flora, architecture, and history.

30] SITE **Devry Institute** / ADDRESS **22801 Roscoe Boulevard, West, Canoga Park, 91304** / ARTIST **David Wilkins, Sylvia Tidwell, and Auston Strauss** / TITLE/DESC **Untitled; architectural element in mixed media** / LOCATION **Exterior and interior** / DATE **1999**

The Devry Institute commissioned David Wilkins to design a sculptural trellis that defines a patio garden area; Austin Strauss to create a collage for the campus library; and then acquired Sylvia Tidwell's "Big Pink," an oil and enamel on canvas.

31] SITE **West Hills Corporate Village** / ADDRESS **8501 N. Fallbrook Avenue, Canoga Park, 91304** / ARTIST **Brad Howe, George Kleiman** / TITLE/DESC **Untitled; acrylic on canvas** / LOCATION **Interior** / DATE **2001**

The Arts Development Fee obligation for West Hills Corporate Village is divided into three parts: 1) Brad Howe created two interior mobile installations in the lobby; 2) Four acrylics on canvas by George Kleiman are located in the concourse of the building lobbies; and 3) A donation to the Fine Art Department of Cal State University Northridge was made to sponsor the CSUN/LAUSD partnership, which sends CSUN students into local public schools to provide arts education.

32] SITE **Northwest Business Park** / ADDRESS **9500-10 Topanga Canyon Boulevard, Chatsworth, 91311** / ARTIST **Laddie John Dill** / TITLE/DESC **Rust Fault; cast concrete sculpture** / LOCATION **Exterior** / DATE **1992**

Laddie John Dill's sculpture incorporates signage and is 7'6" high by 14'6" long by 5' wide at the base and 24" wide at the top. Consistent with the artist's work at the time, the sculpture explores geometrical and geological rock or mountain formations.

33] SITE **Tishman Warner Center** / ADDRESS **6303 Owensmouth, Chatsworth, 91311** / ARTIST **Frank Romero** / TITLE/DESC **History of San Fernando; fountain and fence** / LOCATION **Exterior** / DATE **2000**

After researching the history of the area, Frank Romero created two individual projects, both with the title "The History of San Fernando." The Fountain, approximately 40' long by 6' wide, is inlaid with ceramic tiles depicting different San Fernando motifs. The circular fence—approximately 200' long and 6' high—is made of steel covered in black powdercoat and is thematically similar to the fountain.

34] SITE **Topanga Inn Limited** / ADDRESS **9777 Topanga Canyon Boulevard, Chatsworth, 91311** / ARTIST **Pao Ling Lin** / TITLE/DESC **Untitled; mural: glass; fountain** / LOCATION **Exterior** / DATE **1991**

Artist and architect Pao Ling tells the history of Chatsworth and the Santa Susana pass via a glass mural. The fountain design was based on the rocky formation of the Santa Susana Mountains, incorporating aspects of the mountain environment.

35] SITE **Chatsworth Metrolink Station, Ventura Line** / ADDRESS **Devonshire Street at Canoga Boulevard, Chatsworth, 91311** / ARTIST **John Okulick** / TITLE/DESC **Mountain Passage; painted steel sculpture** / LOCATION **Exterior** / DATE **1997**

Using symbolic imagery, this colorfully painted metal sculpture refers to the station's position as a gateway through the Santa Susanna Pass, from the north into Los Angeles. It visually depicts the history of Chatsworth as a vital link in the development of Los Angeles and areas to the south. This project was jointly commissioned and funded by the MTA and the City of Los Angeles Cultural Affairs Department.

36] SITE **Porter Valley Country Club** / ADDRESS **19216 Singing Hills Drive, Northridge, 91326** / ARTIST **Ed Pinson** / TITLE/DESC **Untitled; wrought iron railings** / LOCATION **Exterior** / DATE **1997**

Porter Valley Country Club commissioned artist Ed Pinson to create designs for the wrought iron railings and other architectural elements of the club to enhance the overall project design.

37] SITE **Porter Ranch Branch Library** / ADDRESS **11371 Tampa Avenue, Northridge, 91326** / ARTIST **Peter Erskine** / TITLE/DESC **Rainbow Sundial Calendar; painted brass medallions and prisms** / LOCATION **Interior** / DATE **1999**

To create this solar art, Peter Erskine used prisms mounted in painted aluminum frames and a solar disk installed into the skylight of the library's central room. Seven brass calendar disks are set in the carpet as guides to various calendar events.

38] SITE **Pacesetter Systems Inc.** / ADDRESS **15900 Valley View Court, Sylmar, 91342** / ARTIST **Various** / TITLE/DESC **Collection; sculpture, paintings and photography** / LOCATION **Interior** / DATE **1992**

The collection consists of work in mixed media such as sculpture, oil on canvas, and photography. It includes work by Bill Wheeler, Kristina Lucas, Martha Chatelain, Mark Kotansky, and Walter Valentini.

39] SITE **Sylmar/San Fernando Metrolink Station** / ADDRESS **Hubbard Avenue at First Street, Sylmar, 91342** / ARTIST **Andro Avedano** / TITLE/DESC **Alegria; sculpture** / LOCATION **Exterior** / DATE **1997**

The 20' by 27' steel sculpture of seven dancing figures is painted in shades of gold and tan on one side, and deep blue on the other. The sculpture is placed directly in front of the Metrolink platform, adjacent to a childcare center. This project was jointly commissioned and funded by the MTA and the City of Los Angeles Cultural Affairs Department.

40] SITE **Eagle Rock 7th Day Adventist** / ADDRESS **2322 Merton Ave., Los Angeles, 90041** / ARTIST **Eustaquio Ines** / TITLE/DESC **Untitled; wood sculpture** / LOCATION **Exterior** / DATE **1993**

The outdoor, wood sculpture of an adult and two children symbolizes the family as a cross-cultural experience while alluding to religious symbols of a church family. The sculpture, located in the main courtyard area, stands over 9' high and is visible and accessible from the street.

41] SITE **MCA/Universal Child Care Center** / ADDRESS **3737 Barnham Boulevard, Universal City, 90068** / ARTIST **Paul Hershfield** / TITLE/DESC **I Dreamed I Was Flying; porcelain enameled steel panels** / LOCATION **Interior** / DATE **1995**

The group of paintings, entitled "I Dreamed I was Flying," was based on the theme of flight, reflecting the wing-like roof and hilltop placement of the architecture. The subject matter was developed to illustrate flight from various perspectives, and the images were chosen and rendered to reflect age-appropriate, cognitive/perceptual abilities.

42] SITE **Winnick Family Children's Zoo** / ADDRESS **5333 Zoo Dr., Los Angeles, 90027** / ARTIST **Armando Alvarez** / TITLE/DESC **Untitled; glass mosaic and steel sculptures** / LOCATION **Exterior** / DATE **2001**

Throughout the Los Angeles Winnick Zoo, several sculptures of powder-coated steel and Byzantine glass mosaic contain themes of children and animals in a consistant color scheme. The central sculpture is a mosaic step-pyramid providing nineteen sensor-activated hand-washing stations. Additional sculptures in the form of silhouettes are placed along the pathways to the petting zoo and at the nursery entrance.

43] SITE **Studio City Branch Library** / ADDRESS **12511 Moorpark Street, Studio City, 91604** / ARTIST **Jacqueline Dreager** / TITLE/DESC **Untitled; bronze sculpture** / LOCATION **Exterior/Interior** / DATE **2001**

Bronze sculptures are placed throughout the exterior and interior of the library grounds. The bronze director's chair in the garden, as well as cast books lying open inside the library, refer to the connection between literature and the film industry.

44] SITE **North Hollywood Police Station** / ADDRESS **11640 Burbank Boulevard, North Hollywood, 91601** / ARTIST **Michael Davis** / TITLE/DESC **Various; steel, glass, granite** / LOCATION **Interior** / DATE **1996**

Michael Davis worked with the station's architects, Meyer & Allen Associates, to create his art plan, which includes four installations. A freestanding façade of steel and glass silkscreened with the image of the old storefront police station stands as the entrance on the public plaza. For the public plaza, he created a paving pattern that incorporates fingerprints. The east-facing entrance wall is installed with granite engraved with the text "to protect and to serve" in both English and Spanish. Inside the building, a glass block wall separating the lobby from the community room encapsulates paraphernalia, text, and objects that demonstrate and visualize behind-the-scenes investigation.

45] SITE **Zerahian Properties** / ADDRESS **4940 Van Nuys Boulevard, Sherman Oaks, 91403** / ARTIST **Debra Malschick, Steven Sorman, Dauna Whitehead, Rita Blitt** / TITLE/DESC **Various; mixed media** / LOCATION **Interior** / DATE **1993**

Malschick's oil and mixed media on canvas is titled "Cortazor's Reoccurring Dream." The mixed-media work by Steven Sorman, entitled "Shoulder," is a limited edition lithograph, woodcut, pigment, bronzing powder and pastel. Dauna Whitehead created two, limited edition cibachrome photographs titled "Echo Park Series." Rita Blitt created a bronze standing sculpture, "Dancing."

46] SITE **Van Nuys / Sherman Oaks Swimming Pool** / ADDRESS **14201 Houston Street, Sherman Oaks, 91423** / ARTIST **John Tucker and Maru Hoeber** / TITLE/DESC **Untitled; bronze sculpture** / LOCATION **Exterior/Interior** / DATE **2001**

The artists produced twenty-five, low-relief bronze sculptures that are embedded in the concrete or attached to the lifeguard towers. The objects range from a forgotten flipper on the trail, to the pool, or a frog on the floor of the shower.

47] SITE **Mitchell Litt** / ADDRESS **14918 Ventura Boulevard, Sherman Oaks, 91403** / ARTIST **Carl Haag** / TITLE/DESC **A Tyrolese Charmois Hunter; painting** / LOCATION **Interior** / DATE **1991**

Mitchell Litt acquired a painting by German artist Carl Haag (1820-1915), "A Tyrolese Chamois Hunter and a Mountain Girl," signed and dated 1858. This watercolor has been exhibited in London, Munich, and Paris.

48] SITE **Signature Group** / ADDRESS **6436 Sepulveda Boulevard, Van Nuys, 91411** / ARTIST **David Venezky** / TITLE/DESC **Untitled; bronze cast plaques** / LOCATION **Exterior** / DATE **1995**

Artist David Venezky created 8 bronze cast plaques depicting in relief four different types of flowering trees, which are planted in this area. The plaques include his personal statements and descriptions of the surrounding foliage, including the names and characteristics of the different species of flowering trees.

49] SITE **Panorama Branch Library** / ADDRESS **14345 Roscoe Boulevard, Panorama City, 91402** / ARTIST **Kim Abeles** / TITLE/DESC **Wall of Knowledge; installation** / LOCATION **Interior** / DATE **1994**

At the entrance to the library, the artist has constructed a doubled sided display case, which is visible from the lobby or from within the library. Chiseled in stone over the display case are the words "Knowledge, Reason, Imagination, Memory," representing the original main categories in the library classification system invented by Melvil Dewey. The display case contains an assemblage of materials related to the making of books.

50] SITE **Edward Kahn** / ADDRESS **11666 Tuxford Street, Sun Valley, 91352** / ARTIST **Frank Nardini** / TITLE/DESC **Untitled; bronze sculpture** / LOCATION **Exterior** / DATE **1992**

Artist Frank Nardini was commissioned to design a sculpture incorporating wildlife, and he chose to depict a trio of swimming dolphins. The sculpture is located in the parking area of Pacific West Investment Co.'s Sun Valley location.

51] SITE **Johnson Building** / ADDRESS **8826 Bradley Avenue, Sun Valley, 91352** / ARTIST **Reis Niemi** / TITLE/DESC **Untitled; iron fence** / LOCATION **Exterior** / DATE **1992**

Building owner Ronald Johnson commissioned artist Reis Niemi to design an iron fence. The piece is ornamental ironwork incorporated in a masonry wall and commercial iron gates, which create the exterior fence of the building.

52] SITE **Al C. Young** / ADDRESS **9111 Sunland Boulevard, Sun Valley, 91352** / ARTIST **Betty Gold** / TITLE/DESC **Untitled; tile mosaic mural** / LOCATION **Exterior** / DATE **1998**

The 30' mosaic tile mural was installed on concrete panels and a roof structure, projecting from the front elevation of an industrial warehouse. Ms. Gold designed the tile mural, using colors that would enhance the building and its surroundings.

53] SITE **Sunland-Tujunga Branch Library** / ADDRESS **7771 Foothill Boulevard, Tujunga, 91042** / ARTIST **Karen Koblitz** / TITLE/DESC **Untitled; tile bench** / LOCATION **Exterior** / DATE **1995**

This outdoor, tile bench is hand painted with images of reptiles, birds, and vegetation of the Sunland-Tujunga Wash. The two-sided bench faces the library on one side and the mountains and park on the other.

54] SITE **Truesdale Recycling & Disposal Center** / ADDRESS **11781 Truesdale Street, Sunland, 91352** / ARTIST **Jacqueline Dreager** / TITLE/DESC **Untitled; sculpture** / LOCATION **Exterior** / DATE **1995**

The artist created a two-part sculpture garden using recycled water meters, copper wire, aluminum wire, computer parts, and other gadgets that are found at recycling centers. Among the sculpture pieces, a large snake poses at the entrance, a bronze globe acts as a working sundial, and benches have been installed for workers. Many of the elements incorporate text in the form of poetry and are thematic to waste and recycling.

55] SITE **Rinaldi Medical Ltd.** / ADDRESS **14901 Rinaldi Street, Mission Hills, 91345** / ARTIST **John Buscemi** / TITLE/DESC **Untitled; metal, glass, and fabric sculpture** / DATE **1994**

John Buscemi's work incorporates images that represent "the expression of healing within the person, society and creation." The sculpture is a mobile; a natural, three-dimensional, kinetic form, which the artist believed was most suitable for the space.

56] SITE **Holy Cross Medical Center** / ADDRESS **15031 Rinaldi Street, Mission Hills, 91345** / ARTIST **Johanna Jordan** / TITLE/DESC **Untitled; water sculpture** / LOCATION **Exterior** / DATE **1993**

Located in the building's atrium, the water sculpture was designed to project an uplifting quality in design and color. It is made of sheet aluminum and painted in automotive lacquer paint.

57] SITE **Greek Marble** / ADDRESS **1600 San Fernando Road, San Fernando, 91340** / TITLE/DESC **Untitled; marble sculpture** / LOCATION **Exterior** / DATE **1995**

Green Marble purchased a white Carrara marble medallion depicting the profile in three-quarter length of Dante Alighieri, the Italian 13th-14th Century Poet and author of the Divine Comedy. The profile is placed within a central circular medallion, encircled by a stepped edge, and flanked by two arched panels with a stepped cornice. The entire pediment is topped with an elaborately carved scrolled acanthus and foliate decoration, retaining the original iron peg supports.

58] SITE **118 Limited Partnership** / ADDRESS **11623 Glenoaks Boulevard, Pacoima, 91331** / ARTIST **Otto "Tito" Sturcke** / TITLE/DESC **Wisdom Guides Her People; tile mosaic mural** / LOCATION **Exterior** / DATE **2001**

"Wisdom Guides Her People" is a mosaic mural measuring 14' x 63' 3" and was commissioned for the new Employment Development Department Building of Pacoima. The artist invoked the theme of wisdom through a female form. She holds the key to the city, which is being handed to a child, while people of different races, age, and eras of the Northeast San Fernando Valley look on. Adorning the four corners of the mural are the California state seal, Los Angeles city seal, California State Assembly seal, and the newly designed Pacoima city seal.

59] SITE **H&R Properties** / ADDRESS **6756-60 Hollywood Boulevard, Los Angeles, 90028** / ARTIST **Michelle Griffoul** / TITLE/DESC **Il Duomo Celeste; ceramic and glass tile mosaic** / LOCATION **Exterior** / DATE **1993**

A ceramic and glass tile mosaic is inset in the dome of this building. The piece is a contemporary interpretation of a celestial scene, which features stars and moons towering above the boulevard.

60] SITE **Panavision Hollywood (McCadden Place Partners)** / ADDRESS **6735 Selma Ave., Los Angeles, 90028** / ARTIST **N/A** / TITLE/DESC **Untitled; movie posters** / LOCATION **Interior** / DATE **1996**

This Hollywood establishment decided to celebrate the great history of the movie industry by restoring and displaying "movie art." Movie posters from well known movies such as "The French Connection" and "Taxi Driver" are placed throughout the building.

61] SITE **Jay E. Silverman** / ADDRESS **1541 N. Cahuenga Boulevard, Los Angeles, 90028** / ARTIST **David Rudolph** / TITLE/DESC **Untitled; sculpture** / LOCATION **Exterior** / DATE **2000**

David Rudolph designed and constructed three relief panels (32"x 18"x 3") cast in white concrete and reinforced with steel. The progression of three panels spans the east-facing wall of the building and portrays the figure of a man in a suit and the perspective of his shadow behind him.

62] SITE **Pick-Vanoff/Sunset Gower Studios** / ADDRESS **1438 N Gower Street, Los Angeles, 90028** / ARTIST **Mark Eric Gulsrud** / TITLE/DESC **Crystal Portal; stained glass and metal gate** / LOCATION **Exterior** / DATE **1994**

A handmade glass archway serves as the entry to the Pick-Vanoff Studios. "Crystal Portal" is of mixed media and incorporates stained glass and metalwork in a unique design, which stands as the Sunset/Gower Studios' signature gate. The portal incorporates neon tubing and stainless steel elements and is Art Deco in style.

63] SITE **Pick Vanoff/Sunset Gower Studios** / ADDRESS **1415 N. Gordon Street, Los Angeles, 90028** / ARTIST **Nancy Kinitsch** / TITLE/DESC **Untitled; decorative painted panels** / LOCATION **Exterior** / DATE **1998**

Eighteen decorative panels were painted in the style of WPA and movie posters. The panels depict the various trades in the movie and television production industry as well as movies and/or characters filmed at the studio.

64] SITE **SK Southern California II** / ADDRESS **4996 Melrose Avenue, Los Angeles, 90029** / ARTIST **Alberto Ossa** / TITLE/DESC **Angels; architectural elements** / LOCATION **Exterior** / DATE **2001**

Alberto Ossa's designs of angels, iron grates, and ceramic tiles were inspired by the original 1926 Walter Allen Plant Rentals Building. Two angels, which frame the corner of the building, are three-dimensional sculptures inspired by the name and identity of Los Angeles. Some of the original (1920s) building materials were retained in the ceramic tiles at the top of the columns. One of the original concrete "angel" faces was used to make a mold that was used to create twenty-four glazed tiles.

65] SITE **John C. Fremont Branch Library** / ADDRESS **6121 Melrose Avenue, Los Angeles, 90036** / ARTIST **Barbara Field** / TITLE/DESC **Big Ideas; sculpture** / LOCATION **Exterior** / DATE **1996**

"Excitement!" and "Inquiry?" greet the visitor to the library through this artist's sculptures. Two free-standing sculptures in the form of an exclamation mark—a symbol of excitement, urgency, results and intellect—and the question mark, symbolizing inquiry, quest, process, and creativity—flank either side of the entrance outside and can be seen from the reading room. A sculpture, in the form of a set of parentheses, embraces an oak tree in the center of the courtyard.

66] SITE **Studio Management Services** / ADDRESS **1040 Las Palmas Avenue, Los Angeles, 90038** / ARTIST **Mitzi Mogul** / TITLE/DESC **Untitled; gate** / LOCATION **Exterior** / DATE **2001**

The entrance gates to Hollywood Center Studios were designed and fabricated in the style of old Hollywood, reminiscent of the Art Deco motif prevalent in many of Hollywood's historic landmarks.

67] SITE **Melrose Enterprises, Inc.** / ADDRESS **7508 Melrose Avenue, Los Angeles, 90046** / ARTIST **Paul Tzanetopoulos** / TITLE/DESC **Try Directional; concrete sidewalk** / LOCATION **Exterior** / DATE **1998**

For the sidewalk bordering 7500 Melrose Avenue, artist Paul Tzanetopoulos designed a pigmented, embossed pattern set directly into the concrete surface. The design incorporates the bus stop, a tree grate, and a new tree into its design.

68] SITE **The Art Store** / ADDRESS **7301 Beverly Boulevard, Los Angeles, 90036** / ARTIST **Victor Henderson** / TITLE/DESC **Untitled; painted mural** / LOCATION **Exterior** / DATE **1992**

The Art Store, a subsidiary of Standard Brands Paint Company, commissioned a mural by artist Victor Henderson. The mural, which consists of eight 4' x 12' panels, depicts the skyline of downtown Los Angeles on life-size scale as if one is looking at the skyline from a high-rise window.

69] SITE **Pan Pacific Park Recreation Center** / ADDRESS **7600 Beverly Boulevard, Los Angeles, 90036** / ARTIST **Jody Zellen** / TITLE/DESC **Untitled; photo and tile mosaic** / LOCATION **Interior/Exterior** / DATE **2001**

Focusing on the history of the Art Deco and Streamline Moderne architecture of Los Angeles, Jody Zellen used photographic images of past and existing buildings. Ceramic tiles are installed on the center's façade and interior walls to mirror the architectural detailing on the building.

70] SITE **Burton Place Retail Center** / ADDRESS **333 S. La Cienega Boulevard, Los Angeles, 90048** / ARTIST **Jose Antonio Aguirre** / TITLE/DESC **Suenos de Primavera and Luna de Octubre; glass mosaic** / LOCATION **Exterior / Date 1993**

The two murals were executed in the traditional techniques of Byzantine glass mosaic and glass mirror mosaic. The theme of these murals was inspired by the Art Deco and Art Nouveau periods reflecting the architectural style of the building. The composition combines visual poetry with some realistic and abstract iconography relating to Japanese woodcuts and designs of the late 19th century and some of the fashion elements of the 1920s.

71] SITE **Robertson Parking Structure** / ADDRESS **123 S. Robertson Boulevard, Los Angeles, 90048** / ARTIST **Rod Baer** / TITLE/DESC **Here Is; metal panel sculpture** / LOCATION **Interior** / DATE **1998**

"Here Is" is a series of twenty-two enameled metal panels forming a poetic reverie of images and text dispersed throughout the parking structure. The sculpture uses the building's physical form of stacking to present a spiraling mirror of meanings and references. As one moves up through the building, each floor presents an increasingly larger system, beginning with the smallest container, our body, then moving through vessel, architecture, city-state, location, and ending with the cosmos.

72] SITE **USAA Realty Co.** / ADDRESS **5055 Wilshire Boulevard, Los Angeles, 90036** / ARTIST **Paul Maxwell** / TITLE/DESC **Structured File/Multiple Events; acrylic on metal painting** / LOCATION **Exterior** / DATE **1992**

The piece is constructed of many layers of painted "screens" with openings of different sizes to reveal what is underneath. The piece symbolizes the systems and instruments by which we try to identify and quantify those aspects of reality which are beyond observation by the naked eye.

73] SITE **Memorial Branch Library** / ADDRESS **4625 W. Olympic Boulevard, Los Angeles, 90019** / ARTIST **William Judson/Judson Studios** / TITLE/DESC **Untitled; stained glass windows** / LOCATION **Interior** / DATE **1996**

In a new, expanded section of the library, the artist created ten individual windows in an English Tudor style, consistent with the original windows created by the artist's great-grandfather. Each panel is designed to represent the ten categories of the Dewey Decimal system: Reference, Religion, Philosophy, Social Science, Language, Science, Technology, Arts, Literature, and History.

74] SITE **Wilshire Police Station** / ADDRESS **4861 Wilshire Boulevard, Los Angeles, 90034** / ARTIST **Roderick Sykes** / TITLE/DESC **Untitled; murals and landscaping** / LOCATION **Interior/Exterior** / DATE 1999

The project at the police station consists of several elements including six murals created through community workshops. The murals are located throughout the station; one is made of glass and ceramic tile, and the others are acrylic on canvas. Additionally, several black and white photographs represent the faces of the community. A landscaped garden area, comprised of native cactus and succulents, volcanic and river rock, oversized machine gears, bottles and other found objects, is located outside the building.

75] SITE **Washington Irving Branch Library** / ADDRESS **4313 W. Washington Boulevard, Los Angeles, 90019** / ARTIST **Elliott Pinkney** / TITLE/DESC **Circle of Knowledge and Book of Discovery; mixed media sculptures** / LOCATION **Interior** / DATE **2001**

Pinkney's first piece, Book of Discovery, resides under the skylight in the lobby. A deep green resin sculpture, it consists of a cone base inscribed with animals, symbols, a male figure, and objects of learning such as a beaker. Above the base are four sculpted faces out of which hands emerge holding an open book. The second piece is a series of free-standing clear acrylic pieces set on a plinth near the information desk. The third piece, Circle of Knowledge, is a disk that hangs against the window near the information desk.

76] SITE **South Los Angeles Animal Care and Control Center** / ADDRESS **3612 11th Avenue, Los Angeles, 90018** / ARTIST **Eloy Torrez** / TITLE/DESC **Untitled; painted mural** / LOCATION **Interior/Exterior** / DATE **2001**

Muralist Eloy Torrez painted four exterior panels and two interior panels on fiberglass mesh. The murals encapsulate the role of the animal care facility in the community, representing the citizens and the importance of proper animal care.

77] SITE **Baldwin Hills Branch Library** / ADDRESS **2906 South La Brea Avenue, Los Angeles, 90016** / ARTIST **Todd Gray** / TITLE/DESC **Untitled; Photo-collage sculpture** / LOCATION **Interior** / DATE **2000**

Todd Gray digitally arranged colorful images into a photo collage of the galaxy and seashells. The dynamic composition sits behind plexiglass in a house-shaped metal frame at the north end of the reading room. A second sculpture, a spiral shape built of copper-colored spheres that range between 6" to 30" in diameter, is suspended over the reference desk.

78] SITE **Robertson Branch Library** / ADDRESS **1719 S. Robertson Boulevard, Los Angeles 90034** / ARTIST **Erika Rothenberg** / TITLE/DESC **Under the Covers; sculpture** / LOCATION **Exterior** / DATE **1998**

The artist, working with building architect Steven Ehrlich, adorned the front facade with a series of quotations about books and learning. Several individuals are quoted, including Malcolm X, Maxine Hong Kingston, Dorothy Parker, Robert Frost, and Oscar Levant.

79] SITE **Hillcrest Promenade Associates** / ADDRESS **9616 Pico Boulevard, Los Angeles 90035** / ARTIST **Frank Romero** / TITLE/DESC **Untitled; painted mural** / LOCATION **Interior** / DATE **1996**

Hillcrest Promenade commissioned artist Frank Romero to paint a mural on the lower two levels of the parking structure of this retail shopping center. The frieze shows a parade humorous cars, ornaments, food and whimsical images.

80] SITE **Venice Crossroads Associates LLC** / ADDRESS **8985 Venice Boulevard, Los Angeles 90034** / ARTIST **Barbara McCarren** / TITLE/DESC **Untitled; lightpoles** / LOCATION **Exterior** / DATE **1997**

In the shopping center parking lot, the artist constructed three lightpoles, each representing a different measuring tool: a scale, a compass, and thermometer.

81] SITE **Sony Pictures Day Care Center** / ADDRESS **3845 Clarington Avenue, Culver City, 90232** / ARTIST **John Okulick** / TITLE/DESC **Fun Zone; fence and gate** / LOCATION **Exterior** / DATE **1994**

Artist John Okulick and architect Steven Ehrlich collaborated on this fence and gate, which incorporate a series of curvilinear shapes and primary colors often found in children's toys. A stage-like framework refers to the Art Deco fencing used around other buildings in the immediate area.

82] SITE **Twentieth Century Fox Film Corporation** / ADDRESS **10201 Pico Boulevard, Los Angeles, 90064** / ARTIST **1] Tony Berlant 2] Rene Petropoulos 3] Horace Bristol** / TITLE/DESC **1] Untitled/mural 2] Untitled/painting 3] Untitled/photographs** / LOCATION **Interior** / DATE **1996**

Tony Berlant's 37' x 8' mural is painted on found and fabricated sheet steel. Whorls of color are applied in layers, create depth and movement. The strikingly colorful image is based on Rupert Murdoch's thumbprint. Rene Petropoulos' piece, entitled "Just What is Your Position" is based on the idea of constant movement. The elliptical, mixed media painting, which spans the wall at 20' x 40', is visible from multiple viewpoints. Horace Bristol's photographs of farmers during the Depression era were used to case the parts in 20th Century Fox Film's "Grapes of Wrath."

83] SITE **West Los Angeles Parking Enforcement Facility** / ADDRESS **11214 Exposition Boulevard, Los Angeles, 90064** / ARTIST **Laura Larson** / TITLE/DESC **Untitled; floor tiles** / LOCATION **Exterior and interior** / DATE **1999**

The artist of this project, working with the building's architects, Nadel Architects, played with iconic traffic symbols, i.e., the hexagon of a stop sign and the triangle of a yield sign. On the exterior of the building, these shapes appear in terra cotta molds inset into the glazed block masonry of the building's façade and are scored into the concrete entryway. Inside, the shapes appear in color—green, red and yellow—and are worked into the tile floor.

84] SITE **Anawalt Lumber Company** / ADDRESS **11060 W. Pico Boulevard, Los Angeles 90064** / ARTIST **Charles Arnoldi** / TITLE/DESC **Crutch; bronze sculpture** / LOCATION **Exterior** / DATE **2001**

Positioned in the parking lot, this bronze sculpture takes the shape of potatoes and makes reference to Anawalt Lumber Company's expanding nursery business. Charles Arnoldi has often characterized nature in his paintings and sculptures, and feels this sculpture complements the hard, linear aspects of the lumber company.

85] SITE **Champion Development Group** / ADDRESS **2206 Sawtelle Boulevard, Los Angeles, 90064** / ARTIST **Michael Flechtner; Eva Cockcroft** / TITLE/DESC **Untitled; neon sculpture** / LOCATION **Exterior** / DATE **1996**

Neon artist Michael Flechtner and muralist Eva Cockcroft created a neon aquarium in an exterior glass tower located on the corner of Olympic and Sawtelle Boulevards. Neon sealife appears in motion, with computerized timing providing random color shifts.

86] SITE **UCLA Credit Union** / ADDRESS **1500 S. Sepulveda Boulevard, West Los Angeles, 90025** / ARTIST **Mark Lere** / TITLE/DESC **Untitled (Sphere Blade); steel sculpture** / LOCATION **Exterior** / DATE **1996**

Lere's piece is a transformed, severed globe. This is one in a series of globes created by Lere, questioning expectations and composition of the world.

87] SITE **Westwood Parking Structure** / ADDRESS **1036 Broxton Avenue, Los Angeles, 90024** / ARTIST **Rod Baer** / TITLE/DESC **Untitled; sculpture and inlay** / LOCATION **Exterior** / DATE **2001**

A life-sized board game winds through the shops and restaurants, which includes the names of streets, arrows and directions, maps, and a "free parking" square inlaid in the concrete "game squares." Scattered throughout the board are three-dimensional game pieces such as dice and compasses, which serve as seating.

88] SITE **California Animal Hospital Inc.** / ADDRESS **1736 S. Sepulveda Boulevard, Los Angeles, 90025** / ARTIST **1] Michael Meaker 2] Kay Finch** / TITLE/DESC **1] Untitled; mural; 2] Untitled; bronze sculptures** / LOCATION **Interior** / DATE **1992**

A bronze Bengal tiger and its base were cast by an unidentified artist between 1910 and 1925. The second bronze sculpture, cast between 1950 and 1959 by Kay Finch, is a bust of a grand champion German Shepherd. In addition to the bronzes, the California Animal Hospital commissioned an original landscape mural by Michael Meaker.

89] SITE **Marcel George Family Trust** / ADDRESS **11800 Wilshire Boulevard, Los Angeles, 90025** / ARTIST **Daniel Keohane** / TITLE/DESC **Bird of Paradise; fountain** / LOCATION **Interior** / DATE **1995**

Bronze birds of paradise form the center piece of artist Daniel Keohane's fountain. The fountain is located in an artist-designed niche within the building lobby.

90] SITE **Pacific Palisades Recreation Center** / ADDRESS **851 Alma Real Drive, Pacific Palisades, 90272** / ARTIST **Barbara McCarren** / TITLE/DESC **Homecourt; sculpture** / LOCATION **Interior** / DATE **2000**

For the Center's lobby, Barbara McCarren created an homage to the community's history and to the traditions of sporting venues. Four retired basketball jerseys are framed with accompanying plaques, which identify four members of the Pacific Palisades community who were part of L.A.'s intellectual movement during the 1930s and 40s.

91] SITE **Champion Development** / ADDRESS **11947 W. Wilshire Boulevard, Los Angeles, 90025** / ARTIST **Michael Fletchtner, Rip Cronk** / TITLE/DESC **Painted Murals—California Classical; Trompe L'oeil Façade; and Art Does Not Read Like a Sentence / Neon Mural—Better Mousetrap** / LOCATION **Exterior** / DATE **2000**

Two artists created a series of exterior murals using two distinctive mediums. Rip Cronk painted three murals in the traditional mural style: "California Classical," "Trompe L'oeil Façade,"and "Art Does Not Read Like a Sentence." Michael Flechtner's piece, "A Better Mousetrap," is non-traditional in its use of neon. The three panel series of animated figures includes "The Gyroscope," "The Dipping Bird," and "The Crab."

92] SITE **Bundy/Olympic Partnership** / ADDRESS **11900 Olympic Boulevard, West Los Angeles, 90064** / ARTIST **Eric Orr** / TITLE/DESC **Untitled; fountain** / LOCATION **Exterior** / DATE **1992**

A bronze water fountain—composed of three vertical obelisks offset from one another —is part of the building's entrance plaza.

93] SITE **Kilroy Realty/Westside Media** / ADDRESS **12200 W. Olympic Boulevard, West Los Angeles, 90064** / ARTIST **Philip Vaughn** / TITLE/DESC **Spiral Fountain Water Sculpture** / LOCATION **Exterior** / DATE **2001**

The design is a series of spiraling, linear pools with a gentle change of elevation that causes water to flow from the outside to the central spiral pool. Dramatic kinetic water patterns travel up and down the spiral line. The pool sits in the center of a circular paving pattern and is nestled into a grass berm.

94] SITE **Chiat/Day/Mojo Inc.** / ADDRESS **340 S. Main Street, Venice, 90291** / ARTIST **Claes Oldenburg and Coosje van Bruggen** / TITLE/DESC **Binoculars; steel sculpture** / LOCATION **Exterior** / DATE **1992**

The four-story high sculpture is the entrance and focal point of its accompanying office building by architect Frank Gehry. The piece consists of steel tube framework clad with reinforcing materials and finished with gray elastomeric paint. Each barrel form contains a small conference room with a skylight window and an oversized light bulb pendant fixture. The artists and architect collaborated closely on the integration of the art into the building design.

95] SITE **Charles Company** / ADDRESS **1501-23 Lincoln Boulevard, Venice, 90291** / ARTIST **Emile Louis Picault** / TITLE/DESC **Honor Patria; bronze sculpture** / LOCATION **Interior** / DATE **1991**

Signed by E. Picault circa 1890, the bronze sculpture of a Roman warrior is located in the lobby of the building.

96] SITE **Venice-Abbot Kinney Branch Library** / ADDRESS **510 S. Venice Boulevard, Venice, 90291** / ARTIST **Betty Dore** / TITLE/DESC **Untitled; mural** / LOCATION **Interior** / DATE **1997**

Dore's three part mural weaves through the two reading rooms and the circulation area. In the children's reading room, a frieze is located above the top of the bookcases, and in the adult reading room, the frieze is composed of "archeological fragments" of written knowledge from past and present cultures, combined with words, letters and symbols. The third piece, in the circulation area, is a mural that represents the connection between Venice, Italy and Venice, California.

97] SITE **Alpha Therapeutic Corporation** / ADDRESS **5555 Valley Blvd., Los Angeles, 90032** / ARTIST **Joe Fay** / TITLE/DESC **Untitled; aluminum sculpture** / LOCATION **Exterior** / DATE **1993**

Joe Fay created two aluminum obelisk sculptures, which stand 10' tall with a 3' concrete base, for the outdoor entrance of the corporation. The sculptures have a brushed aluminum finish and molecular designs that relate to corporate products.

98] SITE **Youth Opportunities Unlimited (Y.O.U) Alternative High School** / ADDRESS **943 W. Manchester Street and 932 W. 85th Street, Los Angeles, 90044** / ARTIST **Michael Massenberg** / TITLE/DESC **Untitled; mural** / LOCATION **Exterior** / DATE **2000**

Using the space over the high school's entryway, the artist painted a mural that depicts education and empowerment. The artist used found and created images to best represent the community, which collaborated with him.

99] SITE **Costa Macaroni** / ADDRESS **4770 E. Valley Boulevard, Los Angeles, 90032** / ARTIST **Judson Studios** / TITLE/DESC **Untitled; stained glass window** / LOCATION **Exterior** / DATE **1996**

From the wheat field to the serving platter, the story of pasta is depicted in the 2'7" x 18" window in the main entry of the Costa Macaroni Manufacturing Company, which was established in 1923.

100] SITE **El Serreno Recreation Center** / ADDRESS **4721 Klamath Street, Los Angeles, 90032** / ARTIST **Elsa Flores** / TITLE/DESC **Untitled; tile mural** / LOCATION **Interior** / DATE **2000**

Recalling her own childhood at the El Serreno swimming pool, “the plunge,” as she refers to it, Flores depicts a community of all generations in carefree play in her mosaic tile mural in the pool area of the recreation center.

101] SITE **Malabar Branch Library** / ADDRESS **2801 Wabash Avenue, Los Angeles, 90033** / ARTIST **Mary Lynn Dominquez, Jesus Dominguez, Ellen Phillips** / TITLE/DESC **Journey** / LOCATION **Interior**

In creating this piece, the artists explored the theme of "journey" through the motif of a maze. Their exploration begins with the image of a clock surrounded by symbols of life's events. From the clock, twelve pathways form a maze-like band of polychrome wood which travels across the library's balcony and fireplace wall. The symbols used on the clock and maze are repeated in sculptural form throughout the library.

102] SITE **Robert Louis Stevenson Branch Library** / ADDRESS **803 Spence Street, Los Angeles, 90023** / ARTIST **Xavier Llongueras** / TITLE/DESC **Nostros Verde Mondo (Our Green World); tile mosaic** / LOCATION **Interior** / DATE **1997**

The vivid colors of this mosaic, above the fireplace, recall the style of the Spanish architect Antonio Gaudi. The center of the mosaic contains a relief figure inspired by Mayan mythology.

103] SITE **Lincoln Heights Branch Library** / ADDRESS **2530 Workman Street, Los Angeles, 90031** / ARTIST **Ricardo Rodriquez Duffy** / TITLE/DESC **Serpent of Knowledge; ceramic tile mural** / LOCAITON **Interior** / DATE **1996**

This piece spans three archways in the lobby, each of which is supported by four columns.

Each column is decorated with a scene depicting a Los Angeles environment. At the top of each column, a plumed serpent/dragon flies through the clouds, an image chose because both symbolize power in two different ancient cultures: Asian and Aztec/Mayan.

104] SITE **Nelson Name Plate Company** / ADDRESS **2800 Casitas Avenue, Los Angeles, 90039** / ARTIST **James Russel** / TITLE/DESC **Scribe; stainless steel fountain** / LOCATION **Exterior** / DATE **1999**

James Russel created a site-specific work to incorporate the fountain and patterned walkway surrounding it. "Scribe" takes its theme from nameplate fabrication.

105] SITE **White Memorial Medical Center** / ADDRESS **1720 E. Cesar Chavez, Los Angeles, 90033** / ARTIST **1] Richard Wyatt 2] Kent Twitchell 3] George Yepe** / TITLE/DESC **Mural series: "L.A. Afternoon;" "Jesus and the Children;" and Untitled** / LOCATION **Exterior and interior** / DATE **1995**

Wyatt's trompe l'oeil mural in the lobby, "L.A. Afternoon," depicts a juxtaposition of ethnically diverse figures and a lush landscape. Kent Twitchell's life-sized mural, "Jesus and the Children," is located in the emergency room and is a memorial in remembrance of the children in the Oklahoma City bombing. George Yepes' mural is on the exterior of the building.

106] SITE **DWP Perimeter Picket Fence** / ADDRESS **1630 N. Main Street, Los Angeles, 90031** / ARTIST **Michael Amescua** / TITLE/DESC **Untitled; Iron fence** / LOCATION **Exterior** / DATE **1996**

The wrought iron fence tops the masonry perimeter fence and is reminiscent of Mexican geometric and the Greek Key designs. At the top of each column on the fence is a design representing a turbine.

107] SITE **Daily Journal** / ADDRESS **915 E. 1st Street, Los Angeles, 90012** / ARTIST **Lorenzo E. Ghiglieri** / TITLE/DESC **Sculpture** / LOCATION **Interior** / DATE **1993**

Developers, Fran Savitch & Associates, Inc. commissioned artist Lorenzo E. Ghiglieri and landscape designer William B. Woods to create an atrium design. The design includes two bronze otters in a natural environment.

108] SITE **Aliso Pico Community Center** / ADDRESS **370 S. Clarence St., Los Angeles, 90033** / ARTIST **Jacki Apple** / TITLE/DESC **Untitled; multimedia installation** / LOCATION **Interior** / DATE **1999**

Artist Jackie Apple created an environmental design treating the lobby as a gallery installation space with seventeen recessed niches arranged in a pattern inspired by music. The artist also helped choose the color palette of blue, green, and yellow.

LIBRARIES

CULTURAL AFFAIRS DEPARTMENT

Over the past six years, the Cultural Affairs Department has advanced projects in twenty-seven Los Angeles Public Library branches. These state-of-the-art facilities include renovated and expanded historic buildings, as well as new buildings designed by many of Los Angeles' finest architects. The art projects range from custom-built furniture to large murals; from skylights to stained glass windows. Many of the artists involved addressed the power of books, libraries, and literacy, and included the respective communities in the creative process.

"The sixty-seven branch libraries and the Central Library of the Los Angeles Public Library are vibrant community centers that offer the most comprehensive array of books and multi-media resources of any library system in the nation. The works of art not only enrich people's experience of these libraries, but the art is also a vivid testament to the cherished role that libraries play in people's lives," according to Susan Kent, City Librarian.

The twenty-seven libraries that have participated in the Cultural Affairs Department Percent for Art program during the latter half of the 1990s have produced an amazing body of work.

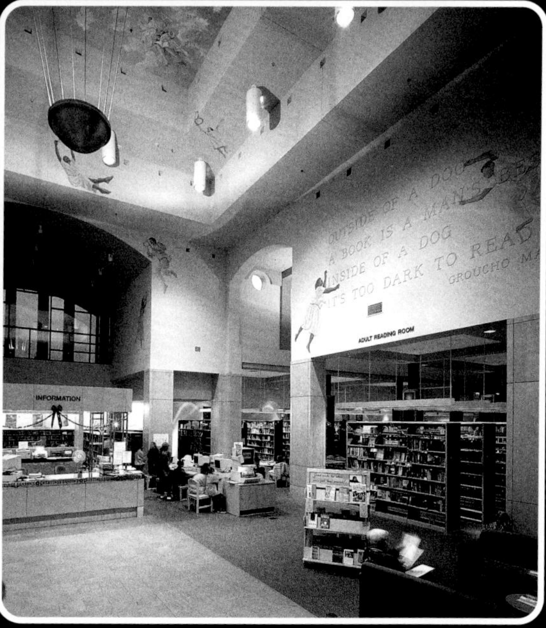

10] MID-VALLEY LIBRARY

109] SITE **Greyhound Station** / ADDRESS **1716 E. 7th Street, Los Angeles, 90021** / ARTIST **Christina Schlesinger** / TITLE/DESC **The Big Splash; painted mural** / LOCATION **Exterior** / DATE **1992**

This is the first work of art financed by the "Percent for Art" program. The large mural faces the outdoor courtyard and depicts a waterfall, a highway, cacti, flowers, and what its artist, Christina Schlesinger, describes as "the spirit of California and the thrill of travel."

110] SITE **Kwan Development** / ADDRESS **752 S. Alameda Street, Los Angeles, 90021** / ARTIST **Cho Yiu Kwan** / TITLE/DESC **Eat It Up; sculptural relief** / LOCATION **Exterior** / DATE **1992**

The sheet metal, wood, and steel frame sculptural relief runs along two sides of the building, and some pieces are approximately 30' above street level, which makes the work visible from the distance.

111] SITE **Julius Giannini (AAA Packing and Shipping)** / ADDRESS **1611E. Washington Blvd., Los Angeles, 90021** / ARTIST **Paul Tzanetopoulos** / TITLE/DESC **Grove 1 and 2; stainless steel sculpture** / LOCATION **Exterior** / DATE **2000**

"Grove 1 and 2" are two 10' faceted, tapered columns placed in a landscape setting. The sculptures amplify and absorb perpetual movement from large semi-truck trailer traffic to the organic swaying of adjacent palms.

112] SITE **San Pedro Development, Inc.** / ADDRESS **1100-1150 S. San Pedro, Los Angeles, 90015** / ARTIST **David Venezky** / TITLE/DESC **Needle Pulling Thread; light sculpture** / LOCATION **Exterior** / DATE **1993**

Attached to the building façade, the stainless steel needle and neon lit thread traverse the top of the building in a wave pattern, finally connecting to a neon spool of thread at the other end of the building. The artist collaborated with the architecture team of J.C. Choi and Steven Chang of EaWes Architects.

113] SITE **Wall Street Garment Center Properties** / ADDRESS **1100-1116 S. Wall Street, Los Angeles, 90015** / ARTIST **1] Jacob Maruisi and David Venezky 2] George Castano Market Day** / TITLE/DESC **1] planters 2] mural** / LOCATION **Exterior** / DATE **1993**

Thirty colorful banners designed and fabricated by artist George Castano are displayed on the exterior walls. In addition, David Venezky created an installation of twenty-six planters along both sides of the building. On the south side of side of the building, a mural depicts a Passi Flora botanical drawing, which is reminiscent of botanical illustrations found in textbooks and encyclopedias.

114] SITE **The City Market Fashion Plaza** / ADDRESS **1122 Wall Street, Los Angeles, 90015** / ARTIST **Mark Lere** / TITLE/DESC **Head to Toe; sandblasted glass** / LOCATION **Exterior** / DATE **1994**

An eight-panel, sandblasted glass installation at the City Market Fashion Plaza reflects the history of fashion. Different shapes and styles within the panels demonstrate the political, social and philosophical influences on changes in fashion.

115] SITE **New Alley Center** / ADDRESS **1220 Santee Street, Los Angeles, 90015** / ARTIST **Joe Fay** / TITLE/DESC **Flock of Birds; aluminum relief wall sculpture** / LOCATION **Exterior** / DATE **1992**

Artist Joe Fay designed and fabricated a wall sculpture depicting a flock of birds in flight. The birds overlap one another in various planes, creating the effect of a three-dimensional relief. The aluminum sculpture is finished to look like polished brass.

116] SITE **Santee Five Partnership** / ADDRESS **1501 Santee Street, Los Angeles, 90015** / ARTIST **Sergia Meiron; sculpture** / LOCATION **Exterior** / DATE **1992**

The artist designed a brass sculpture to be installed over the entrance of the building.

117] SITE **Maa's Holding Company** / ADDRESS **1349 S. Broadway, Los Angeles, 90015** / ARTIST **Barbara Field** / TITLE/DESC **Dream's Peak; mosaic tile mural** / LOCATION **Exterior** / DATE **1994**

The designs for two tile mosaics are site-specific, echo the architecture of the building design, and refer to the rich architectural history of India. The elongated compositions repeat the architect's theme of two columns throughout the building, standing for the father and his two sons. The design is hand-painted onto bisque ceramic tiles.

118] SITE **Bunker Hill East** / ADDRESS **311 S. Spring Street, Los Angeles, 90015** / ARTIST **Lili Lakich** / TITLE/DESC **When The Eagle Flies; neon and metal sculpture** / LOCATION **Interior** / DATE **1991**

Located at the guard desk in the lobby, the neon and metal bas relief uses George Washington as a central theme.

119] SITE **LAPD Metro Emergency Command** / ADDRESS **150 N. Los Angeles Street, Los Angeles, 90012** / ARTIST **B.J. Krivanek** / TITLE/DESC **Untitled; sculpture** / LOCATION **Exterior** / DATE **2001**

Artist B.J. Krivanek created a vortex comprised of a seemingly chaotic arrangement of elliptical columns, each with a dark polished surface. The columns surround one center cylinder made of reflective glass.

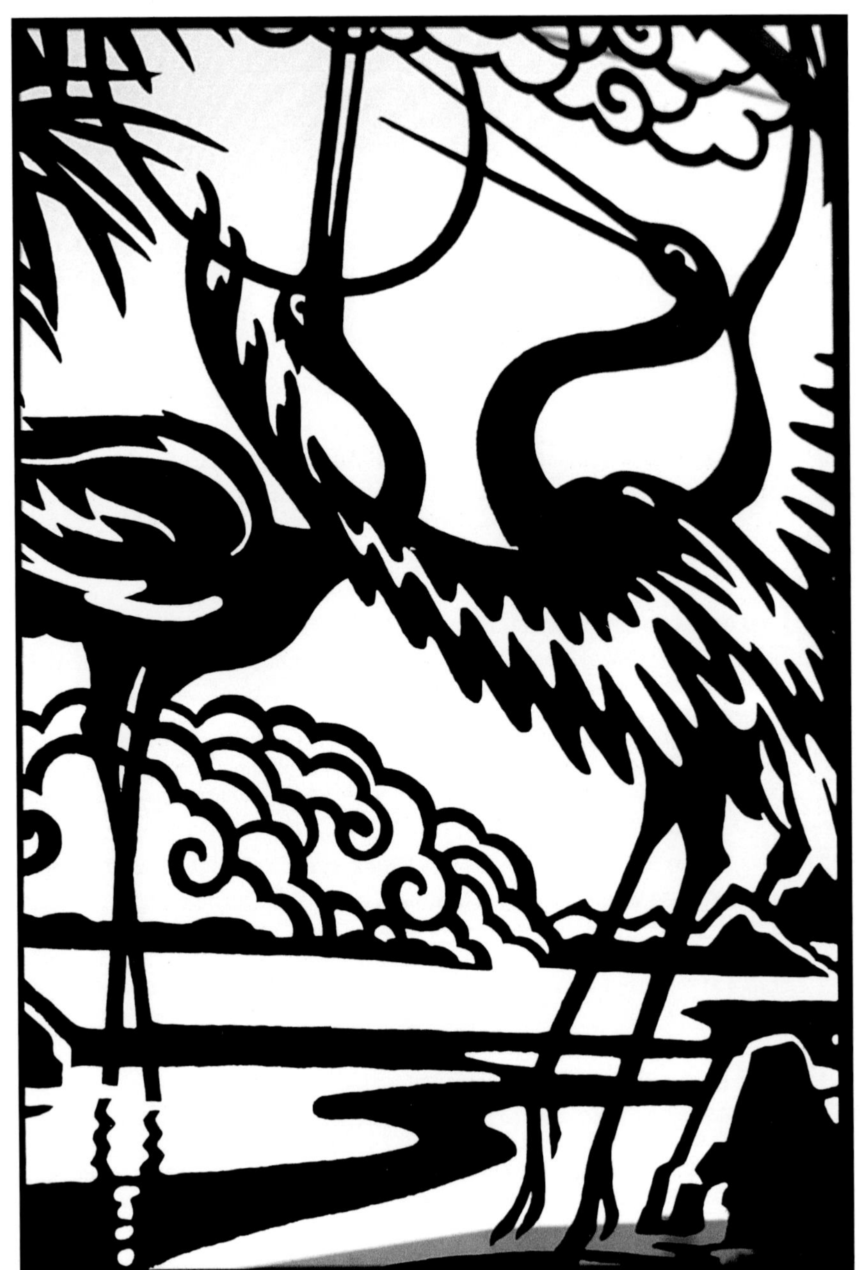

151] SATIN CALIFORNIA

120] SITE **Smith, Hricik & Munselle Development** / ADDRESS **401 S. Boylston Street, Los Angeles, 90017** / ARTIST **Mark Stock** / TITLE/DESC **Enrapture; mural** / LOCATION **Exterior** / DATE **1998**

"Enrapture: Scene One" consists of two, wall-size murals, which are photo-enlargements of paintings printed on vinyl. The first installation of the three-part narrative that will unfold over time, each scene replaces its predecessor.

121] SITE **LA Chamber of Commerce (UC Land Assoc.)** / ADDRESS **350 S. Bixel, Los Angeles, 90017** / ARTIST **1] Simon Toparovsky 2] Billy Al Bengston** / TITLE/DESC **1] Water in the Desert; fountain 2] Aloha LA Bienvendios; painted mural** / LOCATION **Interior** / DATE **1995**

"Water In The Desert" is a water wall constructed of pigmented mortar, bronze, rocks and water plants and contains a working fountain with a pond and live fish and sculpted hands that reach out to the water. "Aloha L.A. Bienvendios" is located in the building lobby. The painted panels are a continuous frieze installed on the main lobby walls.

122] SITE **Echo Park Branch Library** / ADDRESS **1410 W. Temple Street, Los Angeles, 90026** / ARTIST **Alejandro De La Loza** / TITLE/DESC **Untitled; metal relief sculpture** / LOCATION **Interior** / DATE **1997**

Four pieces are located in entrance foyer, with the central piece consisting of a cluster of people. Other pieces incorporate mythical figures and symbols as well as elements common to the community and area.

123] SITE **Shidler Group** / ADDRESS **2600 Wilshire Boulevard, Los Angeles, 90057** / ARTIST **Laddie John Dill** / TITLE/DESC **Tryptych; painting** / LOCATION **Interior** / DATE **1992**

The Shidler Group commissioned artist Laddie John Dill to create a work for the building lobby. Dill's piece complements the marble, stone, and glass building materials.

124] SITE **Saint Vincent Medical Center** / ADDRESS **2200 W. 3rd Street, Los Angeles, 90057** / ARTIST **Richard Wyatt** / TITLE/DESC **View from Saint Vincent; trompe l'oeil mural** / LOCATION **Interior** / DATE **1994**

The large-scale, trompe l'oeil painting, located in the entrance lobby of the hospital, features people of different ages and ethnic groups enjoying a day in the park. In addition to this piece, Saint Vincent Medical Center commissioned several smaller works of art that explore the subject of healing.

125] SITE **Felipe De Neve Branch Library** / ADDRESS **2820 W. 6th Street, Los Angeles, 90020** / ARTIST **Joe Pinkelman and Steven Freedman** / TITLE/DESC **Hollow Wall Diptych; steel sculpture** / LOCATION **Interior** / DATE **1998**

Located in the main reading room, Hollow Wall consists of two steel panels, each of which has been cut through with the lines of a poem. The words are positioned to be read in the left-hand panel, but the words on the right panel are mirrored in reverse.

126] SITE **Fixel Realty** / ADDRESS **2835 W. 9th Street, Los Angeles, 90006** / ARTIST **Mary Barnes** / TITLE/DESC **Untitled; steel sculpture** / LOCATION **Exterior** / DATE **1992**

Mary Barnes collaborated with Angelil/Graham Architecture in order to integrate art and architecture. Their collaboration is the creation of an "urban screen," which is transparent yet protective, and "architectonic" in nature. During business hours, people pass freely through, under, and around the steel screen, causing the piece to mediate the experience of moving between street and building.

127] SITE **Cahuenga Branch Library** / ADDRESS **4591 Santa Monica Boulevard, Los Angeles, 90029** / ARTIST **Victor Henderson and Elizabeth Garrison** / TITLE/DESC **Untitled; painted murals** / LOCATION **Interior** / DATE **1996**

In reading alcoves that flank the building's entrance courtyard off the parking lot, a series of murals creates a narrative that incorporates architectural elements from the original library. For example, two trompe l'oeil paintings of life-size figures, a young boy and a young girl standing in niches, imitate the niches at the entrance of the building. Two main murals form a pair, the subject of one is daytime and the other nighttime, and depict architectural elements as fragments of buildings, symbols of knowledge, and California.

128] SITE **Los Feliz Branch Library** / ADDRESS **1939 Hillhurst, Los Angeles, 90027** / ARTIST **Joyce Dallal** / TITLE/DESC **The Conjunction of 500 Wishes; installation** / LOCATION **Interior** / DATE **1999**

Drawing inspiration from nearby Griffith Park Observatory, the artist extended the concept of "wishing upon a star" to create this installation. The installation covers the four walls of a pyramid shaped dome ceiling topped by a skylight. The artist invited the community to contribute their wishes for the installation.

129] SITE **Wilshire Branch Library** / ADDRESS **149 N. St. Andrew's Place, Los Angeles, 90004** / ARTIST **Edwin Pinson and Debrah Ware** / TITLE/DESC **Painted relief mural** / LOCATION **Interior**

The design of the artists' painted frieze surrounding the skylight reception area was inspired by an element of Allan Ruolf's original 1925 plans for the building that were never realized. The frieze's pattern of mythical animals, some holding open books, emblematically defines the library and reading as a threshold into a magical world, apart from the everyday and surrounding urban environment.

130] SITE **Ralph's Grocery/Ratkovich Development** / ADDRESS **670 S. Western Ave., Los Angeles, 90005** / ARTIST **Cork Marcheschi** / TITLE/DESC **Zephyr; stainless steel, aluminum, neon, and plastic sculpture** / LOCATION **Exterior** / DATE **1996**

Artist Cork Marcheschi created a sculpture that pays homage to the neighborhood's art-deco designs and neon signage, including the adjacent Wiltern Theatre. The sculpture evokes the "theater district" characteristics of the site.

131] SITE **Daehan Plaza** / ADDRESS **966 S. Western, Los Angeles, 90015** / ARTIST **Sue Kim** / TITLE/DESC **Untitled; marble and metal sculpture** / LOCATION **Exterior** / DATE **1994**

Kim chose the L.A. riots of the early 90s as the theme of this sculpture and uses color and the form of two interlocking pieces to communicate her combined message of violence, compassion and harmony,

132] SITE **Moon C Kang/Map Business Group** / ADDRESS **1233-1245 S. Western, Los Angeles, 90006** / ARTIST **Kyong Shin Ko** / TITLE/DESC **Let's Celebrate LA's Diversity; painted mural** / LOCATION **Exterior façade** / DATE **1992**

The mural, "Let's Celebrate L.A.'s Diversity," is based on its location in a neighborhood that represents a cross section of cultural influences: the Korean, Afro-American and Hispanic communities.

133] SITE **Jefferson Branch Library** / ADDRESS **2221 West Jefferson, Los Angeles, 90018** / ARTIST **Todd Gray** / TITLE/DESC **Untitled; photography** / LOCATION **Interior** / DATE **2001**

Three, large-scale photographic pieces in the shape of a ladder, a set of wings, and a nonsensical character, are suspended from the ceiling with steel wire in the main foyer of the library and the children's room. Image and text are composed on the die-cut shapes, which are carefully hung so that, depending on the light source, the text or the images emerge into the foreground.

134] SITE **Newton Police Station** / ADDRESS **3400 S Central Avenue, South El Monte, 91733** / ARTIST **Richard Turner** / TITLE/DESC **Various; sculptures and photographs** / LOCATION **Interior** / DATE **1997**

The art program for the Newton Station consists of a suite of related works in a variety of media located throughout the building. The first piece encountered is a series of light boxes with black and white photos. Next, a hanging sculpture of fine copper mesh, with lighting above, gives the illusion of a light filled basket. Beneath this sculpture is a granite map of the Newton precinct. In the lobby, "The Eclipse of Chaos," consists of a smooth bright copper disk floating across a rough cast iron disk composed of an unruly arrangement of handguns and other weapons. The last piece, in the public area of the station, is a series of black and white photographs from the Los Angeles Public Library archives, which record the history of the neighborhood.

135] SITE **Junipero Serra Library** / ADDRESS **4607 S Main, Los Angeles, 90037** / ARTIST **Jacqueline Alexander** / TITLE/DESC **Sharing Ourselves; installation** / LOCATION **Interior** / DATE **1998**

On each wall of the cove created by the central reading room's skylight, a mural has been painted that features artifacts from different cultures: Asian, African, European, and Indian/Latin. Images of the artifacts are interspersed with portraits of members of the library community.

136] SITE **Vermont Square Branch Library** / ADDRESS **1201 W. 48th Street, Los Angeles, 90057** / ARTIST **Nobuho Nagasawa** / TITLE/DESC **Untitled; steel/glass table and wooden stools** / LOCATION **Interior** / DATE **1996**

The steel framed, glass table in the reference area is sandblasted with titles of books that were banned by libraries and school systems through history. Accompanying the table is a magnifying glass, the lens of which is sandblasted with the image of a fig leaf to symbolize enlightenment. Additionally, the artist created eleven small, wooden stools for the children's reading area. Each stool has the shape of a letter from the word IMAGINATION.

137] SITE **Challengers Boys & Girls Club** / ADDRESS **5029 South Vermont, Los Angeles, 90037** / ARTIST **John Okulick** / TITLE/DESC **Untitled; art fence** / LOCATION **Exterior** / DATE **1999**

John Okulick designed the ornamental fence along the perimeter of the Boys and Girls Club. The purpose was to take a functional and necessary wrought iron fence, which is normally seen as a barrier in the community, and transform it into a friendly, light, and inviting edge to the property.

138] SITE **John Muir Branch Library** / ADDRESS **1005 W 64th Street, Los Angeles, 90044** / ARTIST **James Russell** / TITLE/DESC **Untitled; polished stainless steel sculpture** / LOCATION **Exteroir** / DATE **1997**

A polished stainless steel sculpture rises out of a cast base that incorporates handprints of community members. The contrast of the textured handprints to the smooth, polished surface invites viewers to approach the sculpture.

139] SITE **Angeles Mesa Branch Library** / ADDRESS **2700 W. 52nd Street, Los Angeles, 90043** / ARTIST **Alma Lopez and Noni Olabisi** / TITLE/DESC **Education Is A Basic Human Right; mural** / LOCATION **Interior** / DATE **1997**

Surrounding the fireplace in the main reading room, the statement "Education is a basic human right," which is from Article 7 of the United Nations Rights of Child Declaration, is illustrated through the depiction of two important school desegregation cases. The top of the mural presents the Mendez family, whose suit resulted in a federal court ruling in 1947, which desegregated schools in Southern California. The center of the mural portrays the Brown family, and the U.S. Supreme Court ruling, Brown vs. the Board of Education. The lower portion represents the youth who are protesting for human rights.

140] SITE **Van Ness Child Care Center** / ADDRESS **5720 2nd Avenue, Los Angeles, 90043** / ARTIST **Laura Larson** / TITLE/DESC **Untitled; wood sculpture** / LOCATION **Interior** / DATE **2001**

Larger-than-life wood silhouettes of children playing are attached to walls of the lobby and hallways. Each figure is painted with the topography of a different continent. Icons are overlaid on the topography to represent indigenous populations, native animals, and ancient symbols particular to that place. The center of the lobby floor contains a painted globe.

141] SITE **Home Depot USA** / ADDRESS **12975 Jefferson Boulevard, Culver City, 90232** / ARTIST **Laddie John Dill** / TITLE/DESC **1] Volcanic Glacier 2] Tool Bin; sculptures** / LOCATION **Exterior** / DATE **1994**

The artist chose materials that relate to building and construction. The monumentality of the piece and the intricacy of the design are meant to convey the feeling of being inside a structure as well as viewing the structure from the inside out.

142] SITE **Air Traffic Control Tower (FAA)** / ADDRESS **245 Worldway North, Los Angeles, 90009** / ARTIST **Sheila Kline** / TITLE/DESC **XX Marks the Spot; sculpture** / LOCATION **Exterior** / DATE **1995**

The artist collaborated with the building architects, Siegel/Diamond, to create "a symbol of protection, travel, and information." The oval-shaped work, on the tower's east side, is illuminated with two-stage scenes. The first is a rendition of a radarscope filled with aircraft, and the second scene shows the El Segundo Blue Butterfly, a species native to LAX's nearby sand dunes.

143] SITE **American Airlines, LAX** / ADDRESS **Los Angeles World Airport, Terminal 4, 400 World Way, Los Angeles, 90009** / ARTIST **Susan Narduli** / TITLE/DESC **Terrazzo floor, etched and sandblasted glass** / LOCATION **Interior** / DATE **2001**

Susan Narduli designed a terrazzo floor and a number of artistic elements aiming to capture the spirit of flight. The south-facing window of the main vault is set with dichroic glass. The main vault contains etched and sandblasted glass panels presenting a narrative of aspiration and the understanding of flight. Vignettes of flying machines and notations from aeronautics are set in the terrazzo floor, along with images of prominent figures in the history of flight.

144] SITE **H.B Drollinger Company** / ADDRESS **8824 S. Sepulveda Boulevard, Los Angeles, 90045** / ARTIST **Jean-Luc Beghin** / TITLE/DESC **F/A-18; steel sculpture** / LOCATION **Exterior** / DATE **1996**

The artist, known for his imagery of planes and aviation, created a sculpture which mimics the silhouette of a P-51 Mustang cockpit, an airplane that was designed and manufactured in only one hundred days by North American Aviation in El Segundo in 1940. The piece was developed in conjunction with project "Flight Path," which includes the installation of plaques honoring aviation pioneers.

145] SITE **LA Police Recruitment Training Center** / ADDRESS **5651 W. Manchester Avenue, Los Angeles, 90045** / ARTIST **Wayne Healy with East Los Streetscapers** / TITLE/DESC **Murals** / LOCATION **Exterior/Interior** / DATE **1997**

This work involves both an exterior sculpture court, which includes bronze sculpture, granite columns, bronze plaques, reconfigured hardscape, seating and lighting, and two interior murals, located in the lobby and main hallway. The work is a memorial to the police officers who gave their lives in the line of duty, as well as a recognition to the police officers who earned the Medal of Valor.

146] SITE **IAC Los Angeles** / ADDRESS **5333 W. Imperial Highway, Los Angeles, 90045** / ARTIST **Michael Hayden** / TITLE/DESC **IAC/LAX; holographic sculpture** / LOCATION **Exterior** / DATE **1996**

Michael Hayden's sculpture consists of two identical parts that are a mirror image of each other, stretched across the façade of two buildings and forming an expanse between them. Each part consists of four, triangular, holographic panels that are approximately 6' high and 3' wide at their top edges.

147] SITE **GFS Airport Center** / ADDRESS **1099 S. La Cienega Boulevard, Los Angeles, 90045** / ARTIST **1] Marv Brehm 2] George Baker** / TITLE/DESC **History of Aviation; 1] mural on canvas 2] sculpture** / LOCATION **Interior/Exterior** / DATE **1992**

Artist Marv Brehm's mural on canvas, the "History of Aviation," is mounted on the walls of the lobby. Artist George Baker created a sculpture, which is located in the building's courtyard entrance.

148] SITE **77th Street Police Station** / ADDRESS **235 W. 77th Street, Los Angeles, 90003** / ARTIST **Joe Sam** / TITLE/DESC **Roots of the Community; sculpture** / LOCATION **Interior/Exterior**

The "bird-of-paradise" sculpture and mural use the flowers to represent the strong connection between Los Angeles and Mexico, as well as to symbolize beauty and freedom. In the sculpture, "The Four Families of Humankind," the artist created figures of Africans, Asians, Caucasians and Latinos to illustrate diversity.

149] SITE **Algin Sutton Child Care Center** / ADDRESS **8800 S. Hoover Street, Los Angeles, 90044** / ARTIST **June Edmonds** / TITLE/DESC **Untitled; sculptural fence** / LOCATION **Exterior** / DATE **2001**

The center is surrounded by a 120' long, 7' high, wrought-iron fence. Within the fence are hand-painted details. In 2000, June Edmonds completed another piece for the site —a Venetian glass mosaic mural over the doorway to the swimming pool.

150] SITE **Alma Reaves Wood - Watts Branch Library** / ADDRESS **10205 Compton Avenue, Los Angeles, 90002** / ARTIST **Richard Wyatt** / TITLE/DESC **Painted mural** / LOCATION **Exterior** / DATE **1996**

The painted mural above the library entrance depicts children of the neighborhood dressed in graduation robes and mortarboards in front of library building. Flanking the group of children are images of adults, creating a visual record of the community.

151] SITE **Satin California** / ADDRESS **1435 W. 190th St., Gardena, 90248** / ARTIST **Michael Amescua** / TITLE/DESC **Moonlight Becomes You; steel sculpture** / LOCATION **Exterior** / DATE **1995**

The sculpture, highly visible from the street, is evocative of the hand-carved wood curios that come from Chinese culture, and depicts cranes flying into a serene lake area. The sculpture is placed on a pedestal similar to those of Chinese carved wood curios.

152] SITE **Prentiss & Copley** / ADDRESS **1000 190th Street, Torrance, 90502** / ARTIST **Lou Pearson, Robbie Robbins** / TITLE/DESC **Oceana Sails; steel sculpture** / LOCATION **Exterior** / DATE **2000**

To complement the contemporary new warehouse structure designed by John Cataldo Architects, the artists and the owner chose the sculpture "Oceana Sails" to be placed in the exterior plaza directly in front of the building's main entry.

153] SITE **Trans Pacific Container Corp.** / ADDRESS **920 W. Harry Bridges Boulevard, Wilmington, 90744** / ARTIST **Michael Todd** / TITLE/DESC **Tantric Circle; stainless steel sculpture** / LOCATION **Exterior** / DATE **1985**

The stainless steel sculpture refers to the Hindu myth of creation, death, and re-creation. It also refers to the circumnavigation of the earth. The sculpture is located in a garden court created expressly for sculpture and has a protective windscreen.

S WESTERN AV

154] SITE **Gaffey Street Ventures (Phase II)** / ADDRESS **100 N. Gaffey, San Pedro, 90731** / ARTIST **Brad Howe** / TITLE/DESC **33 Degrees, 44 Minutes, 30 Seconds, North Latitude 118 Degrees, 16 Minutes, 42 Seconds, West Longitude** / LOCATION **Exterior** / DATE **2001**

Oceanographic and celestial navigation instruments such as sextants, protractors, compasses, and their use were the primary influence for the artist. Naval architecture —masts, portholes, crows' nests, sonar arrays, crane booms and winches—completed the physical vocabulary for the concept of the sculpture. This sculpture is a primary navigation aid to anyone whose destination happens to be this facility and a recognizable landmark for anyone visiting the City of San Pedro.

155] SITE **Coast Federal Bank** / ADDRESS **1001 S. Pacific Avenue, San Pedro, 90731** / ARTIST **Michael Schofield** / TITLE/DESC **Untitled; oil paintings** / LOCATION **Interior** / DATE **1995**

The commissioned paintings, located on the wall above the teller line, recognize the local fishing industry as the lifeline of San Pedro and continue the tradition of other paintings in the building.

156] SITE **Assistance League of San Pedro/Palos Verdes** / ADDRESS **1441 W. 8th St., 90732** / ARTIST **Lindsey Dion** / TITLE/DESC **Untitled; stained glass windows** / LOCATION **Exterior** / DATE **1994**

A stained glass art project by artist Lindsay Dion serves as a memorial to a deceased member of the Assistance League of San Pedro/Palos Verdes. The window uses the copper foil method used by Tiffany to create many of his masterpieces.

ARTIST AND ARCHITECT COLLABORATIONS

CULTURAL AFFAIRS DEPARTMENT

The Cultural Affairs Department has made special efforts to foster collaboration between a building's architect and the artist commissioned through the art program. For example, the Sony Pictures Day Care Center project brought artist John Okulick together with architect Steven Ehrlich. Okulick and Ehrlich are friends; in fact, Steven Ehrlich designed the artist's studio. Okulick describes the benefits of collaboration as follows: "When the artist and architect work in conjunction, there is clarity to what is being accomplished and a confidence in choosing the right materials and accuracy in details and surroundings. The artist provides a freedom of form, while the architect establishes the context and provides an application of the artwork to its surroundings. When there is a non-competitive union of expression and a desire to create a satisfying balance of ideas, the results are usually exceptional." Ehrlich speaks highly of the process as well: "On this particular project, I set the solids in place and then John took over and did this playful metalwork. I'm a champion of the process that can go on between artists and architects. I think that it can bring into existence ideas that might not otherwise be created and embrace the unexpected."

The following locations are examples of artist and architect collaboration:

FAA CONTROL TOWER AT LOS ANGELES INTERNATIONAL AIRPORT

NORTH HOLLYWOOD POLICE STATION

SONY DAY CARE CENTER

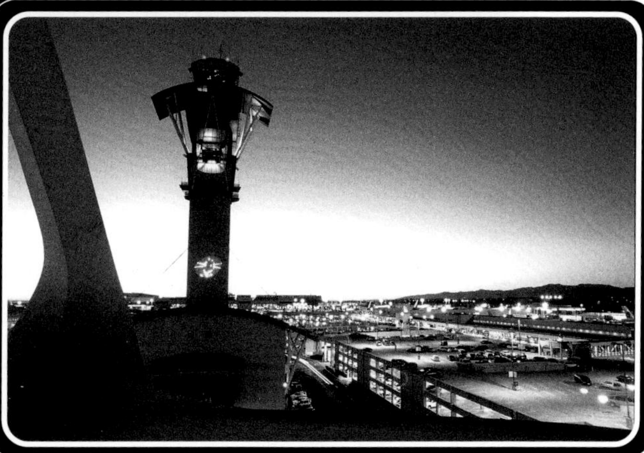

ARTS PROGRAMS

CULTURAL AFFAIRS DEPARTMENT

One of the unique aspects of the City of Los Angeles Cultural Affairs Department public arts program is that its focus is not solely on the visual arts, but rather on all the arts, including music, dance, theatre, film. Moreover, the Cultural Affairs Department program works to extend its effect beyond a single work of art or performance by supporting sustained arts programs. While developers have the option of commissioning a work of art as part of the building site, they also are given the option to extend their support outside the boundaries of a particular building by creating an arts program. These arts programs range from single projects to a series of different projects. They include such projects as sponsoring community cultural events, implementing school programs, and even providing in-kind services to arts groups for much needed, and often ignored, "behind-the-scenes" services, such as providing storage space for theatre groups, or studio rehearsal spaces for performances groups, or offices for arts organizations.

Working with the Cultural Affairs Department, some developers create multifaceted programs that extended to many groups over a period of time. For example, in the Dynamic Builders Arts Program, projects included supporting a jazz festival at Central Avenue High School; sponsoring music workshops at Second Street Elementary school where they also funded repairs to the school piano; and funding the purchase of musical instruments at John Adams Middle School.

The Pep Boys Los Angeles Arts Program also included a variety of projects, one of which was the LAUSD Facilities Enhancement Program involving two schools located near original Pep Boys sites—Welby Way Elementary and Raymond Avenue Elementary. The project's goal was to upgrade the school facilities while enlivening the visual landscape of the school. The selected artists worked with each of the schools' principals to identify images that were meaningful to the school and areas of the campus that were gathering places. At Raymond Elementary School, Jacqueline Alexander created a series of murals for the school's lunch area and handball courts. At Welby Way, Blue McRight created murals for the auditorium and the storage bins. Both artists decided to use the LAUSD standard facilities paint palette, which they found interesting and diverse, in order to incorporate the projects into the fabrics of the schools' facilities and ensure the upkeep of the projects.

Tackling the issue of media literacy, Twentieth Century Fox funded a pilot program created by the International Documentary Association in collaboration with Wonder of Reading, a program based in school libraries. Students were given the opportunity to view a range of documentary films and meet with a film's director/producer to discuss the film and the art of documentary filmmaking. The curriculum included student discussion about the differences between fiction and non-fiction in film, documentaries, news shows, and reality TV. In culminating assignments, students were required to write about the films they had viewed, engaging in the processes of analyzing and critiquing the power and effects of images. A detailed list of Arts Program sponsors is included at the back of the book.

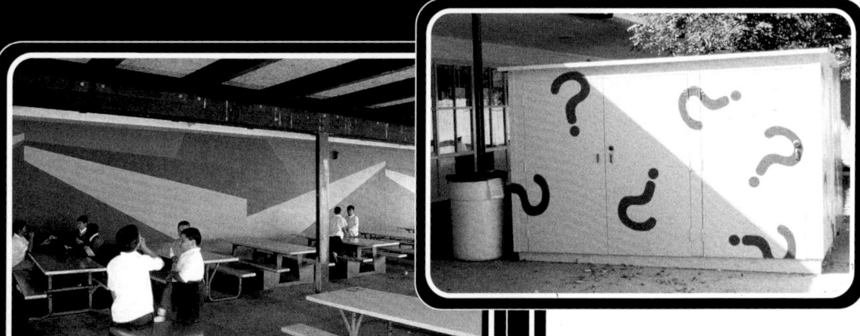

THE COMMUNITY REDEVELOPMENT AGENCY PUBLIC ART PROGRAM

The Community Redevelopment Agency (CRA) of the City of Los Angeles is the prime entity responsible for devising and implementing strategies that serve to reverse deterioration in troubled urban neighborhoods. The CRA directs government and private investment to implement these strategies and takes steps required to promote new investment and growth in these areas.

The CRA's Public Art Program has always been an integral part of the mission of revitalization. Dating back to the late 1960's, the CRA's commitment to the arts was realized on a project-by-project basis. In 1985, a CRA arts policy was formalized for the three downtown redevelopment project areas and in 1993 it was expanded to include all redevelopment areas. Crucial to the existing policy are concepts of community engagement, regional and local artist participation, cultural diversity, "placemaking" to reflect the historical and cultural essence of a community, collaborative design, outreach to and mentoring of artists not current engaged in public art, and artist participation early in the design process. The intention of the policy is to utilize artists and cultural organizations in the revitalization of the LA's neighborhoods.

Projects created as a result of the CRA's efforts have made a major impact on the cultural life of Los Angeles. For example, the CRA provided support resulting in the creation of the Museum of Contemporary Art, the Japanese American Cultural and Community Center, California Plaza's performance spaces, the Central Library and Maguire Gardens, the Los Angeles Convention Center, the Santa Fe Arts Colony, The El Portal Theatre, LA Contemporary Exhibitions, the American Cinemateque/Egyptian Theatre, Inner City Arts, the Museum of African American Art, Grand Hope Park, and others too numerous to list.

The involvement of artists in private and government developments in CRA project areas has brought important works of art into the daily lives of many residents and greatly enhanced our public spaces. Early works include sculptures by artists such as Alexander Calder, Michael Todd, Louise Nevelson, Michael Heizer, and Robert Graham.

As the CRA's commitment to art expanded in the mid-80s, so did the role of artists. Thus, the emphasis shifted towards collaborative design and an inclusion of historians, poets, community members and others who had not typically participated in design efforts. At Grand Hope Park, artists, poets and composers found themselves engaged in creating fountains, benches, wall treatments, pergolas and clock tower chimes. Sheila Levrant de Bretteville added to her design of a sidewalk that wrapped the last remaining block of historic buildings in Little Tokyo the history of each building and business on the block capturing it for us for all time. And in Watts, artist Charles Dickson managed to encapsulate a community's long-held passion for a way to honor Dr. Martin Luther King, Jr. at the site of the 1965 civil disturbances, now a shopping center, by creating a dramatic monument that he titled "Symbols of Unity—The Idea of Freedom."

The CRA is proud of the contributions artists and cultural institutions have made to its efforts to reshape and nourish our great city.

CRA PUBLIC ART

201] SITE **Dr. Martin Luther King, Jr. Shopping Center** / ADDRESS **103rd between Compton & Grandee, Los Angeles, 90002** / ARTIST **Charles Dickson** / TITLE/DESC **Symbols of Unity— The Idea of Freedom; sculpture** / DATE **1992** (NOT MAPPED)

202] SITE **New Otani Hotel & Garden** / ADDRESS **110 S. Los Angeles Street, Los Angeles, 90012** / ARTIST **Gan Iwashiro** / TITLE/DESC **Untitled; sculpture, mexican onyx** / LOCATION **Exterior** / DATE **1977**

203] SITE **Brunswig Square** / ADDRESS **356 E.Second Street, Los Angeles, 90012** / ARTIST **Peter Lodato** / TITLE/DESC **Silver Tower; sculpture** / LOCATION **Exterior** / DATE **1991**

204] SITE **Kaiser Mental Health Facility** / ADDRESS **Chinatown, 765 W. College, Los Angeles, 90012** / ARTIST **Carl F.K. Cheng, Joe Doe Co.** / TITLE/DESC **Water Lens Tower; sculpture** / LOCATION **Exterior** / DATE **1992**

205] SITE **New Otani Hotel & Garden** / ADDRESS **110 South Los Angeles Street, Los Angeles, 90012** / ARTIST **Sentaro Iwaki** / TITLE/DESC **Garden in the Sky; architectural element, garden** / LOCATION **Exterior** / DATE **1977**

206] SITE **Miyako Inn and Spa** / ADDRESS **328 East 1st Street, Los Angeles, 90012** / ARTIST **Susumu Shingu** / TITLE/DESC **Aurora; sculpture, polished stainless steel** / LOCATION **Exterior** / DATE **1986**

207] SITE **The Geffen Contemporary at MoCA** / ADDRESS **152 N. Central, Los Angeles, 90012** / ARTIST **Patrick Bambrough with SCIArc Faculty and students** / TITLE/DESC **The Bike Stops Here; architectural element: bikeracks** / LOCATION **Exterior** / DATE **1996**

208] SITE **Bamboo Plaza** / ADDRESS **988 Hill Street, Los Angeles, 90012** / ARTIST **Dora de Larios** / TITLE/DESC **The Elements; architectural element, entry arch** / LOCATION **Exterior** / DATE **1989**

209] SITE **Promenade Plaza, Bunker Hill** / ADDRESS **710 W. First, 90012** / ARTIST **Sheldon Caris** / TITLE/DESC **Untitled; sculpture, bronze** / LOCATION **Exterior** / DATE **1981**

210] SITE **Sidewalk at Broadway** / ADDRESS **111 S Broadway, Los Angeles, 90012** / ARTIST **Frank Romero** / TITLE/DESC **Untitled; mural, tile** / LOCATION **Exterior** / DATE **1985**

211] SITE **Japanese American National Museum** / ADDRESS **369 E. First Street, Los Angeles, 90012** / ARTIST **Nobuho Nagasawa** / TITLE/DESC **Toyo Miyatake's Camera; sculpture** / LOCATION **Exterior** / DATE **1993**

212] SITE **Weller Court Shopping Center** / ADDRESS **123 S. Weller Court, Los Angeles, 90012** / ARTIST **Shinkichi Tajiri** / TITLE/DESC **Friendship Knot; sculpture, fiberglass** / LOCATION **Exterior** / DATE **1981**

213] SITE **Union Bank of California** / ADDRESS **120 S. San Pedro Street, Los Angeles, 90012** / ARTIST **Seiji Kunishima** / TITLE/DESC **Stone Rise; sculpture, black granite & river boulders** / LOCATION **Exterior** / DATE **1985**

214] SITE **Mitsui Manufacturer's Bank** / ADDRESS **200 S. San Pedro, Los Angeles, 90012** / ARTIST **Jurichiro Hannya** / TITLE/DESC **Peasant Sage of Japan; sculpture, bronze** / LOCATION **Exterior** / DATE **1983**

215] SITE **Little Tokyo Mall** / ADDRESS **319 E. 2nd Street, Los Angeles, 90012** / ARTIST **Michihiro Kosuge** / TITLE/DESC **Towers of Peace, Prosperity & Hope; sculpture** / LOCATION **Exterior** / DATE **1989**

216] SITE **Japanese American Cultural & Community Center** / ADDRESS **244 S. San Pedro Street, Los Angeles, 90012** / ARTIST **Isamu Noguchi** / TITLE/DESC **To The Issei; sculpture, carved basalt & brick** / LOCATION **Exterior** / DATE **1984**

217] SITE **Tokyo Villa** / ADDRESS **222 South Central Avenue, Los Angeles, 90012** / ARTIST **John A. (Tony) Sheets** / TITLE/DESC **Issei No Yume (Issei Dream); sculpture, bronze** / LOCATION **Exterior** / DATE **1987**

218] SITE **330 W.Sunset** / ADDRESS **330 W. Cesar Chavez, Los Angeles, 90012** / ARTIST **Ernesto R. Montano** / TITLE/DESC **Migration; mural** / LOCATION **Exterior** / DATE **1994**

219] SITE **First Street Historic Block** / ADDRESS **120 Judge Jon Aiso to 125 N. Central, Los Angeles, 90012** / ARTIST **Sheila Levrant de Bretteville** / TITLE/DESC **Remembering Old Little Tokyo; installation** / LOCATION **Exterior** / DATE **1996**

220] SITE **Japanese Village Plaza** / ADDRESS **350 E. Second Street, Los Angeles, 90012** / ARTIST **Michael Todd** / TITLE/DESC **Kane Ikebana; sculpture, steel** / LOCATION **Exterior** / DATE **1979**

221] SITE **Honda Plaza** / ADDRESS **400 E. Second Street, Los Angeles, 90012** / ARTIST **Kazuko Mathews** / TITLE/DESC **Thousand Blossoms; mural, ceramic tile** / LOCATION **Exterior** / DATE **1980**

222] SITE **Mitsui Manufacturer's Bank** / ADDRESS **200 S. San Pedro Street, Los Angeles, 90012** / ARTIST **Natalie Kroll** / TITLE/DESC **Origami Horse; sculpture, stainless steel** / LOCATION **Interior** / DATE **1984**

223] SITE **Victor's Clothing Company** / ADDRESS **242 S. Broadway, Los Angeles, 90012** / ARTIST **Neal Taylor and Elaine Fuess** / TITLE/DESC **Seven Roses; mural** / LOCATION **Exterior** / DATE **1996**

224] SITE **Federal Reserve Bank** / ADDRESS **950 S. Grand, Los Angeles, 90012** / ARTIST **Mark Lere** / TITLE/DESC **Untitled; sculptures, steel & copper** / LOCATION **Interior** / DATE **1988**

225] SITE **Los Angeles Garage Associates** / ADDRESS **555 S. Main Street, Los Angeles, 90013** / ARTIST **Frank Romero** / TITLE/DESC **Homage to Downtown Movie Palaces; mural** / LOCATION **Exterior** / DATE **1990**

226] SITE **Biddy Mason Park** / ADDRESS **333 S. Spring, Los Angeles, 90013** / ARTIST **Betye Saar** / TITLE/DESC **Biddy Mason's House of the Open Hand; unknown** / LOCATION **Interior** / DATE **1990**

227] SITE **Biddy Mason Park** / ADDRESS **Broadway & Spring between 3rd & 4th, Los Angeles, 90013** / ARTIST **Sheila Levrant de Bretteville** / TITLE/DESC **Biddy Mason: Time & Place; installation** / LOCATION **Exterior** / DATE **1990**

228] SITE **Pacific Bell/Gas Company Tower** / ADDRESS **433 S. Olive Street, Los Angeles, 90013** / ARTIST **Frank Stella** / TITLE/DESC **Dusk (Mobey Dick series); mural, painted** / LOCATION **Exterior** / DATE **1992**

229] SITE **International Jewelry Center** / ADDRESS **550 S. Hill Street, Los Angeles, 90013** / ARTIST **Michael Hayden** / TITLE/DESC **Generators of the Cylinder; sculpture, argon gas strobe/mecury** / LOCATION **Exterior** / DATE **1982**

230] SITE **Grand Central Square** / ADDRESS **Hill & 3rd, Los Angeles, 90013** / ARTIST **Tim Hawkinson** / TITLE/DESC **Inverted Clocktower; architectural element** / LOCATION **Exterior** / DATE **1994**

231] SITE **Pershing Square Park** / ADDRESS **5th and Olive, Los Angeles, 90013** / ARTIST **Barbara McCarren** / TITLE/DESC **Hey Day; installation** / LOCATION **Exterior** / DATE **1994**

232] SITE **Sidewalk at Broadway** / ADDRESS **330 S. Broadway, Los Angeles, 90013** / ARTIST **Frank Romero** / TITLE/DESC **Tiled Sidewalk; mural, tile** / LOCATION **Exterior** / DATE **1981**

233] SITE **Sidewalk at Broadway & Fourth** / ADDRESS **400 to 424 Broadway, Los Angeles, 90013** / ARTIST **Frank Romero** / TITLE/DESC **Untitled; mural, terra-cotta tile** / LOCATION **Exterior** / DATE **1984**

234] SITE **Figueroa and Olympic** / ADDRESS **Figueroa and Olympic, Los Angeles, 90013** / ARTIST **Michael Tansey** / TITLE/DESC **Daffodil Metamorphosis; sculpture** / LOCATION **Exterior** / DATE **1996**

235] SITE **Broadway Department Stores** / ADDRESS **445 S. Broadway, Los Angeles, 90013** / ARTIST **Diane Gamboa, Leo Limon, Yolanda Gonzalez** / TITLE/DESC **Imagine Unity Broadway; mural** / LOCATION **Exterior** / DATE **1996**

236] SITE **Los Angeles Wholesale Flower** / ADDRESS **755 S. Wall Street, Los Angeles, 90014** / ARTIST **Elizabeth Garrison and Victor Henderson** / TITLE/DESC **Fifty-One Bees; mural** / LOCATION **Exterior** / DATE **1996**

237] SITE **Grand Hope Park** / ADDRESS **510 W. Olympic, Los Angeles, 90015** / ARTIST **Christopher Lee** / TITLE/DESC **Renaissance Weather Station; sculpture: weathervane** / LOCATION **Exterior** / DATE **1994**

238] SITE **The Metropolitan Apartments** / ADDRESS **950 S. Flower Avenue, Los Angeles, 90015** / ARTIST **Dewain Valentine** / TITLE/DESC **Diamond Waterfall; architectural element, fountain** / LOCATION **Exterior** / DATE **1989**

239] SITE **Fashion Institute of Design & Merchandising** / ADDRESS **Grand and 9th, Los Angeles, 90015** / ARTIST **Tony Berlant** / TITLE/DESC **Yang Na; mural** / LOCATION **Interior** / DATE **1990**

240] SITE **Convention Center** / ADDRESS **South Park, Los Angeles, 90015** / ARTIST **Alexis Smith** / TITLE/DESC **Map of the Pacific Rim; Map of the Constellations; architectural elements** / DATE **1993**

241] SITE **Convention Center** / ADDRESS **South Park, Los Angeles, 90015** / ARTIST **Matt Mullican** / TITLE/DESC **Untitled; architectural elements** / DATE **1993**

241A] SITE **Staples Center** / ADDRESS **1111 S. Figueroa, Los Angeles, 90015** / ARTIST **Lloyd Hamrol** / TITLE/DESC **Press; sculpture** / LOCATION **Exterior** / DATE **2000**

241B] SITE **Staples Center** / ADDRESS **1111 S. Figueroa, Los Angeles, 90015** / ARTIST **Mark Lere** / TITLE/DESC **Senses; sculpture** / LOCATION **Exterior** / DATE **2000**

241C] SITE **Staples Center** / ADDRESS **1111 S. Figueroa, Los Angeles, 90015** / ARTIST **Blue McRight** / TITLE/DESC **Garland; sculpture** / LOCATION **Exterior** / DATE **2000**

241D] SITE **Staples Center** / ADDRESS **1111 S. Figueroa, Los Angeles, 90015** / ARTIST **John Outterbridge** / TITLE/DESC **Wing Tips and Angel Eyes at Play; sculpture** / LOCATION **Exterior** / DATE **2000**

241E] SITE **Staples Center** / ADDRESS **1111 S. Figueroa, Los Angeles, 90015** / ARTIST **Jennifer Steinkamp** / TITLE/DESC **X-Ray Eyes; installation** / LOCATION **Interior** / DATE **2000**

242] SITE **Grand Hope Park** / ADDRESS **Grand and Olympic, Los Angeles, 90015** / ARTIST **Lita Albuquerque** / TITLE/DESC **Celestial Source; architectural element, large water** / LOCATION **Exterior** / DATE **1993**

243] SITE **Renaissance Tower** / ADDRESS **501 W. Olympic, Los Angeles, 90015** / ARTIST **Ed Carpenter** / TITLE/DESC **Renaissance Tower Lobby Window; architectural element, glass window** / LOCATION **Exterior** / DATE **1994**

244] SITE **Renaissance Tower** / ADDRESS **501 W. Olympic, Los Angeles,90015** / ARTIST **Christopher Lee** / TITLE/DESC **Light Refractor Rings; sculpture** / LOCATION **Exterior** / DATE **1994**

245] SITE **Renaissance Tower** / ADDRESS **501 S. Grand, Los Angeles, 90015** / ARTIST **Marlo Bartels** / TITLE/DESC **Grand Hope Park Project; installation** / LOCATION **Exterior** / DATE **1994**

246] SITE **The Skyline** / ADDRESS **600 W. Ninth Street, Los Angeles, 90015** / ARTIST **Gary Dwyer** / TITLE/DESC **Angular Unconformity; sculpture, white Carrara** / LOCATION **Exterior** / DATE **1983**

247] SITE **The Skyline** / ADDRESS **600 W. Ninth Street, Los Angeles, 90015** / ARTIST **Guy Dill** / TITLE/DESC **Untitled (Egalmah series); sculpture, precast colored concrete** / LOCATION **Exterior** / DATE **1983**

248] SITE **Grand Hope Park** / ADDRESS **Hope & Olympic, Los Angeles, 90015** / ARTIST **Raul Guerrero with poets Wanda Coleman and Kate** / TITLE/DESC **Mirage Fountain; architectural element, snake fountain** / LOCATION **Exterior** / DATE **1993**

249] SITE **Grand Hope Park** / ADDRESS **South Park, Los Angeles, 90015** / ARTIST **Wanda Coleman** / TITLE/DESC **Many Songs One City/Psalm for the Angels; installation, stenciled scripts** / LOCATION **Exterior** / DATE **1993**

250] SITE **Grand Hope Park** / ADDRESS **Hope & Oympic, Los Angeles, 90015** / ARTIST **Kate Braverman** / TITLE/DESC **The Desert Wind Howls; installation, stenciled script** / LOCATION **Exterior** / DATE **1993**

251] SITE **Grand Hope Park** / ADDRESS **South Park, Los Angeles, 90015** / ARTIST **Raul Guerrero** / TITLE/DESC **Los Angeles Basin circa 1840; architectural, ceramic frieze** / LOCATION **Exterior** / DATE **1993**

252] SITE **Grand Hope Park** / ADDRESS **South Park, Los Angeles, 90015** / ARTIST **Raul Guerrero** / TITLE/DESC **Ancient Fossils; architectural element, bench** / LOCATION **Exterior** / DATE **1993**

253] SITE **Grand Hope Park** / ADDRESS **Hope & Olympic, Los Angeles, 90015** / ARTIST **Raul Guerrero** / TITLE/DESC **Aviary; installation, bird stencils** / LOCATION **Exterior** / DATE **1993**

254] SITE **Grand Hope Park** / ADDRESS **South Park, Los Angeles, 90015** / ARTIST **Raul Guerrero** / TITLE/DESC **Birds of the Southwest; stencils on trellis** / LOCATION **Exterior** / DATE **1993**

255] SITE **Fashion Institute of Design & Merchandising** / ADDRESS **919 S. Grand Avenue, Los Angeles, 90015** / ARTIST **Gwynn Murrill** / TITLE/DESC **sculpture** / LOCATION **Exterior** / DATE **1990**

256] SITE **Renaissance Tower** / ADDRESS **Grand and Hope, Los Angeles, 90015** / ARTIST **Christopher Lee** / TITLE/DESC **Renaissance Turbine; architectural element** / LOCATION **Exterior** / DATE **1994**

257] SITE **Hope and Olympic** / ADDRESS **South Park, Los Angeles, 90015** / ARTIST **Adam Leventhal** / TITLE/DESC **Esperanza Gardens; architectural element** / LOCATION **Exterior** / DATE **1997**

258] SITE **Citicorp Plaza** / ADDRESS **725 S. Figueroa, Los Angeles, 90017** / ARTIST **April Greiman with poet Lucille Clifton** / TITLE/DESC **Walk Earth Talk; architectural element, granite pavers** / LOCATION **Exterior** / DATE **1992**

259] SITE **International Bank of California** / ADDRESS **888 S. Figueroa Street, Los Angeles, 90017** / ARTIST **Eugene Sturman** / TITLE/DESC **Homage to Cabrillo: Venetian Quadrant; sculpture, stainless steel** / LOCATION **Exterior** / DATE **1985**

260] SITE **801 Tower** / ADDRESS **801 Figueroa Street, Los Angeles, 90017** / ARTIST **Andrew Leicester** / TITLE/DESC **Zanja Madre; architectural element, garden/plaza** / LOCATION **Exterior** / DATE **1992**

261] SITE **Los Angeles Wholesale Produce** / ADDRESS **Central & 800, Los Angeles, 90021** / ARTIST **Thomas Suriya** / TITLE/DESC **Los Angeles Wholesale Produce Market; mural, acrylic paint** / LOCATION **Exterior** / DATE **1986**

262] SITE **Metro Gardens** / ADDRESS **Hollywood Blvd and Western, Los Angeles, 90027** / ARTIST **Adam Leventhal** / TITLE/DESC **Dream Walk Fence; architectural element** / LOCATION **Exterior** / DATE **1991** (NOT MAPPED)

263] SITE **Hollywood Bowl Self Storage** / ADDRESS **1847 N. Argyle Avenue, Hollywood 90028** / ARTIST **Rodger Boyce** / TITLE/DESC **Untitled; mural** / LOCATION **Exterior** / DATE **1990** (NOT MAPPED)

264] SITE **Cherokee Whitley Parking Structure** / ADDRESS **1718 N. Cherokee, Los Angeles, 90028** / ARTIST **Kim Yasuda** / TITLE/DESC **Ascent; installation** / LOCATION **Exterior** / DATE **1994** (NOT MAPPED)

265] SITE **Los Angeles Public Library** / ADDRESS **550 S. Hope Street, Los Angeles, 90071** / ARTIST **Lita Albuquerque** / TITLE/DESC **Site/Memory/Reflection; architectural elements** / DATE **1993**

266] SITE **Los Angeles Public Library** / ADDRESS **630 W. Fifth, Los Angeles, 90071** / ARTIST **Rene Petropoulos** / TITLE/DESC **Painting with Multiple Centers; painting** / LOCATION **Interior** / DATE **1993**

267] SITE **Los Angeles Public Library** / ADDRESS **630 W. Fifth, Los Angeles, 90071** / ARTIST **Reis Niemi** / TITLE/DESC **Literate Fence; architectural elements** / LOCATION **Exterior** / DATE **1993**

268] SITE **Los Angeles Public Library** / ADDRESS **630 W. Fifth, Los Angeles, 90071** / ARTIST **Therman Statom** / TITLE/DESC **Natural, Technological, Ethereal** / LOCATION **Interior**/ DATE **1993**

269] SITE **Citibank Center, Bunker Hill** / ADDRESS **444 S. Flower Street, Los Angeles, 90071** / ARTIST **Mark Di Suvero** / TITLE/DESC **Shoshone; sculpture, painted steel** / LOCATION **Exterior** / DATE **1981**

270] SITE **Citibank Center, Bunker Hill** / ADDRESS **444 S. Flower Street, Los Angeles, 90071** / ARTIST **Frank Stella** / TITLE/DESC **Long Beach; sculpture, painted aluminum** / LOCATION **Exterior** / DATE **1982**

271] SITE **Grand Hope Park** / ADDRESS **South Park, Los Angeles, 90071** / ARTIST **Gwynn Murrill** / TITLE/DESC **Urban Curiosity; sculpture, bronze** / LOCATION **Exterior** / DATE **1993**

272] SITE **Citibank Center, Bunker Hill** / ADDRESS **444 S. Flower Street, Los Angeles, 90071** / TITLE/DESC **Michael Heizer** / TITLE/DESC **North, East, South, West; sculpture, polished stainless steel** / LOCATION **Exterior** / DATE **1981**

273] SITE **Los Angeles Public Library** / ADDRESS **630 W. Fifth, Los Angeles, 90071** / ARTIST **Ann Preston** / TITLE/DESC **Illumination; architectural element, lamps** / LOCATION **Interior** / DATE **1993**

274] SITE **Los Angeles Public Library** / ADDRESS **630 W. Fifth, Los Angeles, 90071** / ARTIST **David Bunn** / TITLE/DESC **A Place for Everything and Everything in Its Place; installation** / LOCATION **Interior** / DATE **1993**

275] SITE **Los Angeles Public Library** / ADDRESS **630 W. Fifth, Los Angeles, 90071** / ARTIST **Laddie John Dill and Mineo Mizuno** / TITLE/DESC **Unititled; architectural element, fountain** / LOCATION **Exterior** / DATE **1993**

276] SITE **Union Bank Plaza, Bunker Hill** / ADDRESS **445 S. Figueroa Street, Los Angeles, 90071** / ARTIST **Jerome Kirk** / TITLE/DESC **Aquarius; sculpture, stainless steel** / LOCATION **Exterior** / DATE **1970**

277] SITE **Westin Bonaventure Hotel** / ADDRESS **404 S. Figueroa Street, Los Angeles, 90071** / ARTIST **Dean Gillete** / TITLE/DESC **Earth, Air, Fire & Water; mural, acrylic paint on canvas** / LOCATION **Interior** / DATE **1977**

278] SITE **Stuart M. Ketchum, Downtown YMCA** / ADDRESS **401 S. Hope Street, Los Angeles, 90071** / ARTIST **Milton Hebald** / TITLE/DESC **Olympiade '84; sculpture, bronze** / LOCATION **Exterior** / DATE **1986**

279] SITE **bp Plaza** / ADDRESS **333 South Hope Street, Los Angeles, 90071** / ARTIST **Woods Davy** / TITLE/DESC **Sierra Leone, Verdugo, Covina; sculpture, steel & granite** / LOCATION **Exterior** / DATE **1986**

280] SITE **Los Angeles Marriott Downtown** / ADDRESS **333 S. Figueroa Street, Los Angeles, 90071** / ARTIST **Richard Thomas** / TITLE/DESC **Untitled Fountain; sculpture, clear acryllic tubes** / LOCATION **Exterior** / DATE **1984**

281] SITE **Los Angeles World Trade Center** / ADDRESS **350 S. Figueroa Street, Los Angeles, 90071** / ARTIST **John A. (Tony) Sheets** / TITLE/DESC **The History of World Commerce; architectural element** / LOCATION **Interior** / DATE **1974**

282] SITE **South Hope Street** / ADDRESS **655 S. Hope Street, Los Angeles, 90071** / ARTIST **Laddie John Dill** / TITLE/DESC **Untitled; sculpture, mixed media** / LOCATION **Interior** / DATE **1986**

283] SITE **bp Plaza** / ADDRESS **333 S. Hope Street, Los Angeles, 90071** / ARTIST **Alexander Calder** / TITLE/DESC **Four Arches; sculpture, painted steel** / LOCATION **Exterior** / DATE **1974**

284] SITE **South Hope Street** / ADDRESS **655 S. Hope Street, Los Angeles, 90071** / ARTIST **Richard Rowley** / TITLE/DESC **Charlotte B.; sculpture, aluminum with etching** / LOCATION **Exterior** / DATE **1986**

285] SITE **Los Angeles Public Library** / ADDRESS **630 W. Fifth, Los Angeles, 90071** / ARTIST **Jud Fine** / TITLE/DESC **Spine; architectural element** / LOCATION **Exterior** / DATE **1993**

286] SITE **Stuart M. Ketchum, Downtown YMCA** / ADDRESS **401 S. Hope Street, Los Angeles, 90071** / ARTIST **Gidon Graetz** / TITLE/DESC **Mind, Body, and Spirit; sculpture, stainless steel & bronze** / LOCATION **Exterior** / DATE **1986**

287] SITE **Arco Plaza** / ADDRESS **Financial Core, Los Angeles, 90071** / ARTIST **Herbert Bayer** / TITLE/DESC **Double Ascension; sculpture, painted steel** / LOCATION **Exterior** / DATE **1973**

288] SITE **Mellon Bank Center** / ADDRESS **400 South Hope Street, Los Angeles, 90071** / ARTIST **Alexander Liberman** / TITLE/DESC **Ulysses; sculpture** / LOCATION **Exterior** / DATE **1988**

289] SITE **Grand Promenade** / ADDRESS **255 S Grand, Los Angeles, 90071** / ARTIST **Michael Davis** / TITLE/DESC **Grand Promenade Torcheres; architectural element, lamp standards** / LOCATION **Exterior** / DATE **1988**

290] SITE **Hope Street at 17th** / ADDRESS **Hope Street at 17th, Los Angeles, 90071** / ARTIST **Blue McRight and Warren Wagner** / TITLE/DESC **The Garden of Conversion; sculpture and landscape** / LOCATION **Exterior** / DATE **1996**

291] SITE **Figueroa Towers** / ADDRESS **660 S. Figueroa, Los Angeles, 90071** / ARTIST **Terry Schoonhoven** / TITLE/DESC **City Above; architectural element; ceiling** / LOCATION **Exterior** / DATE **1989**

292] SITE **The Court, Wells Fargo Center** / ADDRESS **333 S. Grand Avenue, Los Angeles, 90071** / ARTIST **Jean Dubuffet** / TITLE/DESC **Le Dandy; sculpture, painted fiberglass** / LOCATION **Interior** / DATE **1982**

293] SITE **The Court, Wells Fargo Center** / ADDRESS **333 S. Grand Avenue , Los Angeles, 90071** / ARTIST **Robert Graham** / TITLE/DESC **Crocker Fountain Figures—Numbers 1, 2 , 3 & 4; sculpture, bronze** / LOCATION **Interior** / DATE **1984**

294] SITE **The Court, Wells Fargo Center** / ADDRESS **333 S. Grand Avenue, Los Angeles, 90071** / ARTIST **Joan Miro** / TITLE/DESC **La Caresse d'un Oiseau; sculpture, painted bronze** / LOCATION **Interior** / DATE **1967**

295] SITE **The Court, Wells Fargo Center** / ADDRESS **333 S. Grand Avenue, Los Angeles, 90071** / ARTIST **Nancy Graves** / TITLE/DESC **Sequi; sculpture, bronze with polychrome** / LOCATION **Exterior** / DATE **1985**

296] SITE **The Court, Wells Fargo Center** / ADDRESS **333 S. Grand Avenue, Los Angeles, 90071** / ARTIST **Louise Nevelson** / TITLE/DESC **Night Sail; sculpture, painted aluminum & steel** / LOCATION **Exterior** / DATE **1985**

297] SITE **Citibank Center, Bunker Hill** / ADDRESS **444 S. Flower Street, Los Angeles, 90071** / ARTIST **Robert Rauschenberg** / TITLE/DESC **Fargo Podium; sculpture, mixed media collage** / LOCATION **Exterior** / DATE **1982**

298] SITE **Sanwa Bank** / ADDRESS **601 S. Figueroa Street, Los Angeles, 90071** / ARTIST **Eric Orr** / TITLE/DESC **L.A. Prime Matter; scultpure, fire/water column** / LOCATION **Exterior** / DATE **1991**

299] SITE **Citibank Center, Bunker Hill** / ADDRESS **444 S. Flower Street, Los Angeles, 90071** / ARTIST **Bruce Nauma** / TITLE/DESC **Trench, Shafts, Pit, Tunnel & Chambers; sculpture, corten steel** / LOCATION **Exterior** / DATE **1982**

300] SITE **Citicorp Plaza** / ADDRESS **725 S. Figueroa, Los Angeles, 90071** / ARTIST **Joe Fay with poet Gary Soto** / TITLE/DESC **Natural Instincts; sculpture** / LOCATION **Exterior** / DATE **1992**

301] SITE **Figueroa Towers** / ADDRESS **660 S. Figueroa, Los Angeles, 90071** / ARTIST **Joyce Kozloff** / TITLE/DESC **Gardens at Villandry and Chenonceaux; mural, Italian glass mosaic panels** / LOCATION **Exterior** / DATE **1989**

302] SITE **Stuart M. Ketchum, Downtown YMCA** / ADDRESS **401 S. Hope Street, South Pasadena, 90071** / ARTIST **Milton Hebald** / TITLE/DESC **Handstand; sculpture, bronze** / LOCATION **Exterior** / DATE **1986**

303] SITE **Library Tower, One Bunker Hill** / ADDRESS **633 W. Fifth, Los Angeles, 90071** / ARTIST **Robert Graham** / TITLE/DESC **Source Figure; sculpture, fountain** / LOCATION **Exterior** / DATE **1992**

304] SITE **Library Tower, One Bunker Hill** / ADDRESS **633 W. Fifth, Los Angeles, 90071** / ARTIST **Vitaly Komar and Alexander Melamid** / TITLE/DESC **Unity; murals and sculpture** / DATE **1992**

305] SITE **Bunker Hill** / ADDRESS **Fourth Street at Grand Avenue, Los Angeles, 90071** / ARTIST **Lloyd Hamrol** / TITLE/DESC **Uptown Rocker; sculpture, reinforced concrete & painted** / LOCATION **Exterior** / DATE **1986**

306] SITE **Citicorp Plaza** / ADDRESS **725 S. Figueroa, Los Angeles, 90071** / ARTIST **Terry Allen with poet Philip Levine** / TITLE/DESC **Corporate Head; sculpture** / LOCATION **Exterior** / DATE **1992**

307] SITE **Manulife Tower** / ADDRESS **865 S. Figueroa, Los Angeles, 90071** / ARTIST **Elyn Zimmerman** / TITLE/DESC **Lithos; architectural element, waterfalls** / LOCATION **Interior/Exterior** / DATE **1991**

308] SITE **Citicorp Plaza** / ADDRESS **725 S. Figueroa, Los Angeles, 90071** / ARTIST **David Gilhooly with poet Robert Mezey** / TITLE/DESC **The Public Abandons Philosphy; Pigeons Acquire Philosophy; sculpture, bronze** / LOCATION **Exterior** / DATE **1992**

309] SITE **Citicorp Plaza** / ADDRESS **725 S. Figueroa, Los Angeles, 90071** / ARTIST **George Herms with poet Charles Simic** / TITLE/DESC **Portals to Poetry; sculpture, assemblage** / LOCATION **Exterior** / DATE **1992**

310] SITE **Citicorp Plaza** / ADDRESS **725 S. Figueroa, Los Angeles, 90071** / ARTIST **James Surls with poet Robert Creeley** / TITLE/DESC **Once There Was a Forest; architectural element, benches** / LOCATION **Exterior** / DATE **1992**

311] SITE **Mesa Street Car Park** / ADDRESS **San Pedro, 90731** / ARTIST **Vicki Scuri** / TITLE/DESC **Mesa Street Car Park; mural** / LOCATION **Exterior** / DATE **1997**

312] SITE **Pacific Place** / ADDRESS **250 W 6th Street, San Pedro, 90731** / ARTIST **Michael Davis** / TITLE/DESC **Navis; fountain and 3 sculptural elements** / LOCATION **Exterior** / DATE **1990** (NOT MAPPED)

313] SITE **The Academy of Television Arts and Sciences** / ADDRESS **5220 N. Lankershim Blvd, North Hollywood 91601** / ARTIST **Kenny Schneider** / TITLE/DESC **Whirligigs; sculpture** / LOCATION **Interior** / DATE **1994** (NOT MAPPED)

313A] SITE **The Academy of Television Arts and Sciences** / ADDRESS **5220 N. Lankershim Blvd, North Hollywood 91601** / ARTIST **Marlo Bartels** / TITLE/DESC **Untitled; architectural elements** / LOCATION **Exterior** / DATE **1992**

313B] SITE **The Academy of Television Arts and Sciences** / ADDRESS **5220 N. Lankershim Blvd, North Hollywood 91601** / ARTIST **Ernest Shelton** / TITLE/DESC **Lucille Ball, Jack Benny, Johnny Carson; sculptures, bronze** / LOCATION **Exterior** / DATE **1992**

313C] SITE **The Academy of Television Arts and Sciences** / ADDRESS **5220 N. Lankershim Blvd, North Hollywood 91601** / ARTIST **Richard Ellis** / TITLE/DESC **Walter Cronkite, George Burns/Gracie Allen, Steve Allen; bas-reliefs** / LOCATION **Exterior** / DATE **1992**

313D] SITE **The Academy of Television Arts and Sciences** / ADDRESS **5220 N. Lankershim Blvd, North Hollywood 91601** / ARTIST **Robert Jacobs** / TITLE/DESC **Ed Sullivan; sculpture, bronze** / DATE **1992**

314] SITE **Hewlett Packard** / ADDRESS **5161 Lankershim Boulevard, North Hollywood, 91601** / ARTIST **Michael Davis** / TITLE/DESC **The Pool and the Landscape; sculpture** / LOCATION **Exterior** / DATE **1985** (NOT MAPPED)

MTA METRO ART

The County of Los Angeles covers over 4,000 square miles—larger than the states of Delaware and Rhode Island combined. In addition to the City of Los Angeles, the County houses eighty-seven other cities, each with their own city council. The Los Angeles County Metropolitan Transportation Authority (MTA) is responsible for working with all these cities to improve mobility throughout the entire region.

The MTA has developed a wide range of transportation programs and services which are aimed at ensuring the County doesn't become a giant parking lot. These programs include Los Angeles' new and expanding Metro Rail system which currently includes 50 operating stations, an additional 40+ are in various stages of planning or construction. On an average weekday, the Metro Rail system serves nearly 250,000 patrons and ridership is rising dramatically.

The benefits of a rail transit system in Los Angeles are manifold. In addition to the speed, efficiency, and environmental benefits, the Metro Rail stations themselves are fast becoming a source of pride to County residents. The stations feature the work of a wide range of talented artists commissioned to create works specifically for the transit system.

The MTA Board has adopted a policy which allocates a percentage of overall rail construction budgets to the enhancement of the rail system through the arts. Works have also been commissioned for the Metro Bus and Metro Rapid systems. Metro Art also supports another local transportation agency with the incorporation of public art into their regional commuter rail system, Metrolink.

Artists have worked as members of multidisciplinary design teams as well as been commissioned to install work into existing environments. The aim has been to transform transportation facilities into something more than concrete loading zones and dull waiting areas. The artwork in the Metro system covers a broad range of styles and mediums and includes such elements as recycled film reels, enormous rock sculptures and archeological artifacts recovered during construction. Light and space and even performance are other artistic mediums employed in the station designs.

MTA Metro Art has received several design and artistic excellence and is recognized for its interdisciplinary approach, the broad range of artists selected, and its innovative and successful community involvement processes. Strong support has been demonstrated by municipal and corporate contributions and by the respect and care given the works by the public.

All artworks are created especially for the transit system and must meet safety, accessibility, and maintenance requirements. Artists are selected through a highly respected peer review process with community input. The remarkably low level of vandalism in the stations is a reflection of the strong sense of community pride in the projects and results in reduced maintenance costs.

The appeal of the Metro Rail system's artwork is enduring. In fact, tours of the Metro Rail artwork led by volunteer docents have an impressive waiting list! Artists continue to play a significant role in shaping Los Angeles and it is clear that an inviting, attractive waiting environment is a strong contributor to the success of our public transit systems.

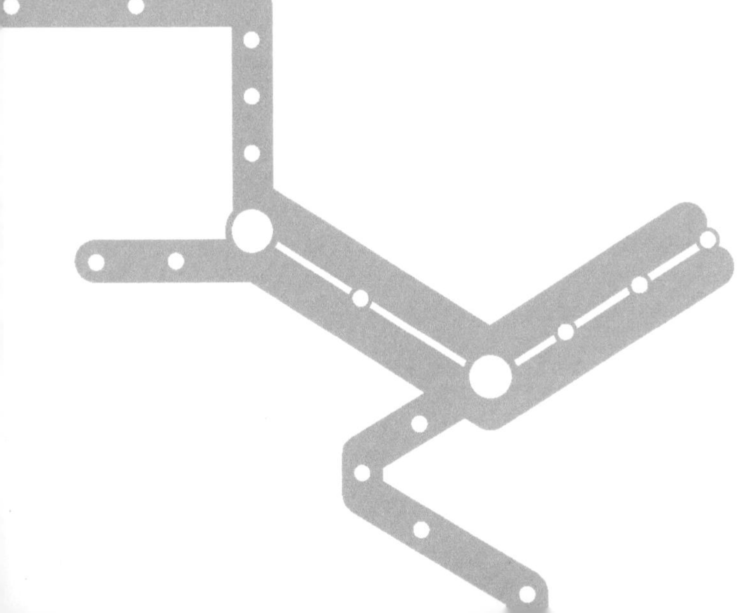

METRO RAIL SYSTEM

401] SITE **7th Street/Metro Center Station** / ARTIST **Joyce Kozloff** / TITLE/DESC. **The Movies: Fantasies and Spectacles; tile mural** / LOCATION **Exterior** / DATE **1993**

402] SITE **7th Street/Metro Center Station** / ARTIST **Roberto Gil de Montes** / TITLE/DESC. **Heaven to Earth; ceramic tile triptych** / LOCATION **Flower Street entrance** / DATE **1993**

403] SITE **7th Street/Metro Center Station** / ARTIST **Terry Schoonhoven** / TITLE/DESC. **City Above; painted ceiling mural** / LOCATION **Exterior** / DATE **1993**

404] SITE **7th Street/Metro Center Station** / ARTIST **Patsy Norvell** / TITLE/DESC. **Glass Passage; etched glass & gold leaf** / LOCATION **Exterior** / DATE **1991**

405] SITE **Tunnel between 7th St./Metro Center and Pico Stations** / ARTIST **Thomas Eatherton** / TITLE/DESC. **Unity; fiberoptic sculpture** / LOCATION **Interior** / DATE **1993**

406] SITE **Pico/Convention Center Station** / ARTIST **Robin Brailsford** / TITLE/DESC. **Time and Presence; painted steel cutouts** / LOCATION **Exterior** / DATE **1993**

407] SITE **Grand Station** / ARTIST **Mark Lere** / TITLE/DESC. **Who, What, Where?; sandblasted text** / LOCATION **Exterior** / DATE **1994**

408] SITE **San Pedro Station** / ARTIST **Sandra Rowe** / TITLE/DESC. **Hope, Dream, Path, Focus, Belief; stainless steel cutouts** / LOCATION **Exterior** / DATE **1993**

409] SITE **Washington Station** / ARTIST **Elliott Pinkney** / TITLE/DESC. **Running for the Blue Line; steel cutout panels** / LOCATION **Exterior** / DATE **1995**

410] SITE **Vernon Station** / ARTIST **Horace Washington** / TITLE/DESC. **A Tribute to Industry; seating sculptures & paving** / LOCATION **Exterior** / DATE **1994**

411] SITE **Slauson Station** / ARTIST **East Los Streetscapers** / TITLE/DESC. **South Central Codex; ceramic tile & porcelain enamel** / LOCATION **Exterior** / DATE **1995**

412] SITE **103rd Street/Kenneth Hahn Station** / ARTIST **Roberto Salas** / TITLE/DESC. **Blue Line Totems in Red; perforated painted steel totems** / LOCATION **Exterior** / DATE **1994**

413] SITE **Rosa Parks (Imperial/Wilmington) Station** / ARTIST **JoeSam.** / TITLE/DESC. **Hide-n-Seek; painted steel figures** / LOCATION **Exterior** / DATE **1995**

414] SITE **Compton Station** / ARTIST **Eva Cockcroft** / TITLE/DESC. **Compton: Past Present & Future; ceramic tile murals** / LOCATION **Exterior** / DATE **1995**

415] SITE **Artesia Station** / ARTIST **Lynn Aldrich** / TITLE/DESC. **Blue Line Oasis; tile mosaic** / LOCATION **Exterior** / DATE **1996**

416] SITE **Del Amo Station** / ARTIST **Colin Gray** / TITLE/DESC. **Del Amo Wheel; cast stone sculpture** / LOCATION **Exterior** / DATE **1999**

417] SITE **Wardlow Station** / ARTIST **Jacqueline Dreager** / TITLE/DESC. **Great Gathering Place; bronze & fiberglass sculptures** / LOCATION **Exterior** / DATE **1992**

418] SITE **Willow Station** / ARTIST **Ann Preston** / TITLE/DESC. **Finding the Way; under construction** / LOCATION **Exterior** / DATE **1999**

419] SITE **Pacific Coast Highway Station** / ARTIST **Joe Lewis** / TITLE/DESC. **Twelve Principles; ceramic tile and aluminum** / LOCATION **Exterior** / DATE **1994**

420] SITE **Anaheim Station** / ARTIST **Terry Braunstein** / TITLE/DESC. **Local Odysseys; photo-montage on porcelain enamel** / LOCATION **Exterior** / DATE **1994**

421] SITE **Fifth Street Station** / ARTIST **Jim Isermann** / TITLE/DESC. **Failed Ideals; stained glass** / LOCATION **Exterior** / DATE **1995**

422] SITE **First Street Station** / ARTIST **Paul Tzanetopoulos** / TITLE/DESC. **Breezy and Delightful; kinetic sculptures** / LOCATION **Exterior** / DATE **1994**

423] SITE **Transit Mall Station** / ARTIST **Patrick Mohr** / TITLE/DESC. **Angel Train; brass and aluminum sculpture** / LOCATION **Exterior** / DATE **1995**

424] SITE **Pacific Station** / ARTIST **June Edmonds** / TITLE/DESC. **We Know Who We Are; glass mosaic** / LOCATION **Exterior** / DATE **1995**

425] SITE **Marine/Redondo Station** / ARTIST **Carl Cheng with Escudero-Fribourg Architects** / TITLE/DESC. **Museum of Space Information; multiple art elements & landscaping** / LOCATION **Exterior, multiple levels** / DATE **1995**

426] SITE **Douglas/Rosecrans** / ARTIST **Renee Petropoulos with Escudero-Fribourg Architects** / TITLE/DESC. **Untitled; multiple art elements & landscaping** / LOCATION **Exterior, multiple levels** / DATE **1995**

427] SITE **El Segundo/Nash Station** / ARTIST **Daniel Martinez with Escudero-Fribourg Architects** / TITLE/DESC. **For Your Intellectual Entertainment; multiple art elements** / LOCATION **Exterior, multiple levels** / DATE **1995**

428] SITE **Mariposa/Nash Station** / ARTIST **Charles Dickson with Escudero-Fribourg Architects** / TITLE/DESC. **Divine Order; multiple art elements** / LOCATION **Exterior, multiple levels** / DATE **1995**

429] SITE **Aviation/I-105 Station** / ARTIST **Richard Turner with Escudero-Fribourg Architects** / TITLE/DESC. **Untitled; multiple art elements and landscaping** / LOCATION **Exterior, multiple levels** / DATE **1995**

430] SITE **Hawthorne/I-105 Station** / ARTIST **Mineko Grimmer with Caltrans architect** / TITLE/DESC. **Companions; bronze sculptures & granite benches** / LOCATION **Exterior, multiple levels** / DATE **1995**

431] SITE **Crenshaw/I-105 Station** / ARTIST **Buzz Spector with Caltrans architect** / TITLE/DESC. **Crenshaw Stories; mosaic** / LOCATION **Exterior, multiple levels** / DATE **1995**

432] SITE **Vermont/I-105 Station** / ARTIST **Kim Yasuda, Torgen Johnson, with Caltrans architect** / TITLE/DESC. **real green; multiple art elements** / LOCATION **Exterior, multiple levels** / DATE **1995**

433] SITE **Harbor Freeway/I-105 Station** / ARTIST **Steve Appleton with Caltrans architect** / TITLE/DESC. **Locus: City Imprints; multiple art elements** / LOCATION **Exterior, multiple levels** / DATE **1995**

434] SITE **Avalon/I-105 Station** / ARTIST **John Outterbridge with Caltrans architect** / TITLE/DESC. **Pyramid; concrete & tile sculpture** / LOCATION **Exterior, plaza level** / DATE **1995**

435] SITE **Avalon/I-105 Station** / ARTIST **Willie Middlebrook with Caltrans architect** / TITLE/DESC. **Portrait of My People #619; porcelain enamel mural** / LOCATION **Exterior, plaza level** / DATE **1995**

436] SITE **Avalon/I-105 Station** / ARTIST **Stanley Wilson with Caltrans architect** / TITLE/DESC. **Bridge of Culture; steel cut outs, ceramic tile** / LOCATION **Exterior, platform level** / DATE **1995**

437] SITE **Long Beach/I-105 Station** / ARTIST **Sally Weber with Caltrans architect** / TITLE/DESC. **Celestial Chance; multiple art elements** / LOCATION **Exterior, multiple levels** / DATE **1995**

438] SITE **Lakewood/I-105 Station** / ARTIST **Erika Rothenberg with Caltrans architect** / TITLE/DESC. **Wall of UnFame; concrete wall & seating panels** / LOCATION **Exterior, multiple levels** / DATE **1995**

439] SITE **I-605/I-105 Station** / ARTIST **Meg Cranston with Caltrans architect** / TITLE/DESC. **Suka: Place of the Bees; fiberglass sculpture & multiple art elements** / LOCATION **Exterior, multiple levels** / DATE **1995**

440] SITE **Union Station** / ARTIST **Christopher Sproat** / TITLE/DESC. **Union Chairs; granite benches** / LOCATION **Interior** / DATE **1993**

441] SITE **Union Station** / ARTIST **Cynthia Carlson** / TITLE/DESC. **LA: City of Angels; painted aluminum** / LOCATION **Interior** / DATE **1993**

442] SITE **Union Station** / ARTIST **Terry Schoonhoven** / TITLE/DESC. **Traveler; ceramic tile mural** / LOCATION **Interior** / DATE **1993**

443] SITE **Civic Center Station** / ARTIST **Jonathan Borofsky** / TITLE/DESC. **I Dreamed I Could Fly; fiberglass sculpture, sound element** / LOCATION **Interior** / DATE **1993**

444] SITE **Pershing Square Station** / ARTIST **Stephen Antonakos** / TITLE/DESC. **Neons for Pershing Square; neon sculpture** / LOCATION **Interior** / DATE **1993**

445] SITE **Westlake/Mac Arthur Park Station** / ARTIST **Therman Statom** / TITLE/DESC. **Into the Light; glass sculptures** / LOCATION **Interior** / DATE **1993**

446] SITE **Westlake/Mac Arthur Park Station** / ARTIST **Francisco Letelier** / TITLE/DESC. **El Sol/La Luna; tile mural** / LOCATION **Interior** / DATE **1993**

447] SITE **Wilshire/Vermont Station** / ARTIST **Peter Shire, with Engineering Management** / TITLE/DESC. **Los Angeles Seen; painted sculptures, skylights** / LOCATION **Exterior/Interior** / DATE **1996**

448] SITE **Wilshire/Normandie Station** / ARTIST **Frank Romero** / TITLE/DESC. **Festival of Masks Parade; mural** / LOCATION **Exterior** / DATE **1996**

449] SITE **Wilshire/Western Station** / ARTIST **Richard Wyatt** / TITLE/DESC. **People Coming, People Going; ceramic tile murals** / LOCATION **Interior** / DATE **1996**

450] SITE **Vermont/Beverly Station** / ARTIST **George Stone with Anil Verma Associates, architect** / TITLE/DESC. **GFRC sculptures** / LOCATION **Exterior/Interior** / DATE **1999**

451] SITE **Vermont/Santa Monica Station** / ARTIST **Robert Millar with Ellerbe-Becket architect** / TITLE/DESC. **space, text, fluorescent light** / LOCATION **Interior (entrance)** / DATE **1999**

452] SITE **Vermont/Sunset Station** / ARTIST **Michael Davis with Diedrich Architects & Associates** / TITLE/DESC. **multiple art elements** / LOCATION **Exterior/Interior** / DATE **1999**

453] SITE **Hollywood/Western Station** / ARTIST **May Sun with Escudero-Fribourg Architects** / TITLE/DESC. **multiple art elements** / LOCATION **Exterior/Interior** / DATE **1999**

454] SITE **Hollywood/Vine Station** / ARTIST **Gilbert "Magu" Lujan with Miralles Associates, architect** / TITLE/DESC. **multiple art elements** / LOCATION **Exterior/Interior** / DATE **1999**

GATEWAY TRANSIT CENTER

Gateway Transit Center is a multi-modal transit center on the east side of the historic Union Station.

455] SITE **MTA Headquarters Building** / ARTIST **James Doolin** / TITLE/DESC. **Los Angeles Circa 1870, 1910, 1960, after 2000; large scale paintings** / LOCATION **Interior (plaza & 3rd level lobbies)** / DATE **1995**

456] SITE **MTA Headquarters Building** / ARTIST **Patrick Nagatani** / TITLE/DESC. **Epoch; large painting** / LOCATION **Interior (Board Room entrance)** / DATE **1995**

457] SITE **MTA Headquarters Building** / ARTIST **Margaret Neilsen** / TITLE/DESC. **L.A. Dialogs; large painting** / LOCATION **Interior (cafeteria entrance)** / DATE **1995**

458] SITE **Corner Park** / ARTIST **Robert Gil de Montes, Elsa Flores, Peter Shire** / TITLE/DESC. **Paseo Cesar Chavez; water fountains & ceramic tile** / LOCATION **Exterior** / DATE **1995**

459] SITE **East Portal to Union Station** / ARTIST **May Sun, Richard Wyatt, Paul Diez** / TITLE/DESC. **City of Dreams, River of History; multiple art elements** / LOCATION **Exterior/Interior** / DATE **1995**

460] SITE **Patsaouras Transit Plaza** / ARTIST **East Los Streetscapers** / TITLE/DESC. **La Sombra del Arroyo; ceramic tile, bronze, concrete** / LOCATION **Exterior** / DATE **1995**

461] SITE **Patsaouras Transit Plaza** / ARTIST **Kim Yasuda, Torgen Johnson, Noel Korten, Matthew Vanderborgh** / TITLE/DESC. **ReUnion; 6 bus shelters** / LOCATION **Exterior** / DATE **1995**

462] SITE **Gateway Transit Center** / ARTIST **Michael Amescua** / TITLE/DESC. **Guardians of the Track; decorative metalwork** / LOCATION **Exterior** / DATE **1995**

463] SITE **Gateway Transit Center; East Portal Entrance to Union Station** / ARTIST **Bill Bell;** / TITLE/DESC. **A-Train; vertical light units, interactive sound** / LOCATION **Interior** / DATE **1995**

METROLINK SYSTEM

Metrolink is a five county commuter rail system owned and operated by the Southern California Regional Rail Authority. MTA Metro Art coordinates a matching grant program for LA County cities interested in enhancing their Metrolink station with art.

464] SITE **Cal State LA Station, San Bernadino Line** / ARTIST **Terry Schoonhoven** / TITLE/DESC. **The Muralists; mural** / LOCATION **Exterior** / DATE **1994**

465] SITE **El Monte Station, San Bernadino Line** / ARTIST **Victor Henderson and Elizabeth Garrison** / TITLE/DESC. **Lions of El Monte; steel cutouts, benches, text** / LOCATION **Exterior** / DATE **1996**

466] SITE **Baldwin Park Station, San Bernadino Line** / ARTIST **Judith Baca with Siegel Diamond architects** / TITLE/DESC. **Danza Indigenas; installation** / LOCATION **Exterior** / DATE **1993**

467] SITE **Pomona Station, San Bernardino Line** / ARTIST **William Attaway** / TITLE/DESC. **Past, Present, Future; installation** / LOCATION **Exterior** / DATE **1997**

468] SITE **Claremont Station, San Bernadino Line** / ARTIST **Rod Baer** / TITLE/DESC. **Conductor's Pocket Watch, Loose Rivets; sculpture** / LOCATION **Exterior** / DATE **1994**

469] SITE **Chatsworth Station, Ventura Line** / ARTIST **John Okulick** / TITLE/DESC. **Mountain Passage; painted steel sculpture** / LOCATION **Exterior** / DATE **1997**

470] SITE **Glendale Station, Santa Clarita Line** / ARTIST **Lynn Goodpasture** / TITLE/DESC. **Tree of Peace; glass mosaic clock** / LOCATION **Exterior** / DATE **1999**

471] SITE **Northridge Station, Ventura Line** / ARTIST **William Nettleship** / TITLE/DESC. **City and Country; concrete relief panels and paving** / LOCATION **Exterior** / DATE **2000**

472] SITE **Sylmar/San Fernando Station, Santa Clarita Line** / ARTIST **Andro Avedano** / TITLE/DESC. **Alegria; sculpture** / LOCATION **Exterior** / DATE **1997**

473] SITE **Santa Clarita Station, Santa Clarita Line** / ARTIST **Viqui McCaslin** / TITLE/DESC. **Share the Earth with Others; handmade tile mural** / LOCATION **Exterior** / DATE **1995**

474] SITE **Sun Valley Station, Santa Clarita Line** / ARTIST **Paul Tzanetopoulos** / TITLE/DESC. **mosaic tile wall** / LOCATION **Exterior** / DATE **2001**

WHERE THE ART IS

EAST

S BRAND BLVD
S CHEVY CHASE DR
GLEN
40
EAGLE ROCK BLVD
YORK BLVD
MISSION ST
N AVE 54
LOS FELIZ BLVD
128
RIVERSIDE DR
FRANKLIN AV
HOLLYWOOD BLVD
N SAN FERNANDO RD
N FIGUEROA ST
6263
MONTEREY RD
VINE ST
127
SILVER LAKE BLVD
GLENDALE BLVD
HUNTINGTON DR N
MELROSE AV
64
N VERMONT AV
104
103
N BROADWAY
PASADENA FRWY
129
ALHAMBRA AV
98
97
100
HOLLYWOOD FRWY
W 3RD ST
122
N SPRING ST
106
99
DALY ST
VALLEY BLVD
125
124
130
123
126
121
120
W 6TH ST
1ST ST
119
SAN BERNARDINO FRWY
131
S ALVARADO ST
118
105
101
4TH ST
107
E 1ST ST
132
W OLYMPIC BLVD
108
CESAR E CHAVEZ AV
W WASHINGTON BLVD
S HOOVER ST
117
115
113
7TH ST
109
E 4TH ST
S WESTERN AV
S VERMONT AV
114
112
110
POMONA FRWY
E 3RD ST
S FIGUEROA ST
S GRAND AV
S MAIN ST
116
OLYMPIC BLVD
WHITTIER BLVD
102
133
S SAN PEDRO ST
SANTA ANA FRWY
111
S ATLANTIC BLVD
EXPOSITION BLVD
134
MARTIN LUTHER KING JR BLVD
E 37TH ST
S SOTO ST
E WASHINGTON BLVD
W VERNON AV
135
E VERNON AV
136
BANDINI BLVD
HARBOR FRWY
137
139
140
S SANTA
PACIFIC
EASTERN AV
TRAL AV
W SLAUSON AV
AV

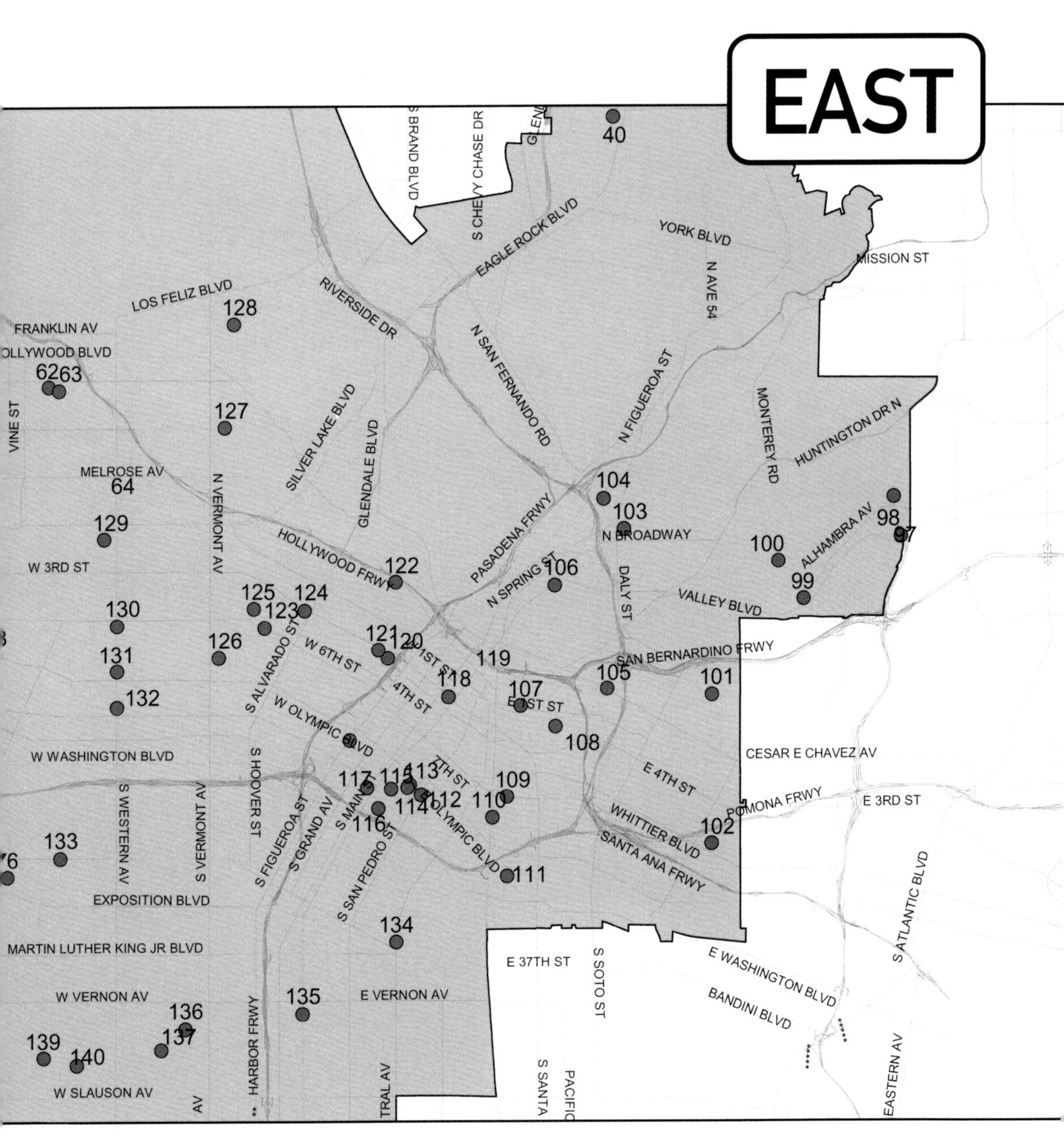

FOOTHILL FRWY
LITTLE TUJUNGA RD
SAN FERNANDO RD
POLK ST
SAN DIEGO FRWY
57
58
FOOTHILL BLVD
GLENOAKS BLVD
56
55
S BRAND BLVD
FOX ST
VAN NUYS BLVD
OSBORNE ST
WENTWORTH ST
53
54
VESPER AV
OSBORNE ST
SAN FERNANDO RD
52
SUNLAND BLVD
LA TUNA CANYON RD
SHELDON ST
TUXFORD ST
51
PARTHENIA ST
49
WEBB AV
50
HONOLULU AV
VANOWEN ST
48
VINELAND AV
LAUREL CANYON BLVD
N HOLLYWOOD WY
N BUENA VISTA ST
VICTORY PL
N GLENOAKS BLVD
WOODMAN AV
E OLIVE AV
N SEPULVEDA BLVD
BURBANK BLVD
44
W MAGNOLIA BLVD
W GLENOAKS BLVD
MAGNOLIA BLVD
45
46
W OLIVE AV
W ALAMEDA AV
WESTERN AV
HOLLYWOOD WY
LANKERSHIM BLVD
47
43
MOORPARK ST
W BROADWAY
W COLORADO ST
41
BEVERLY GLEN BLVD
MULHOLLAND DR
S GLENDALE AV
42
LOS FELIZ BLVD
59

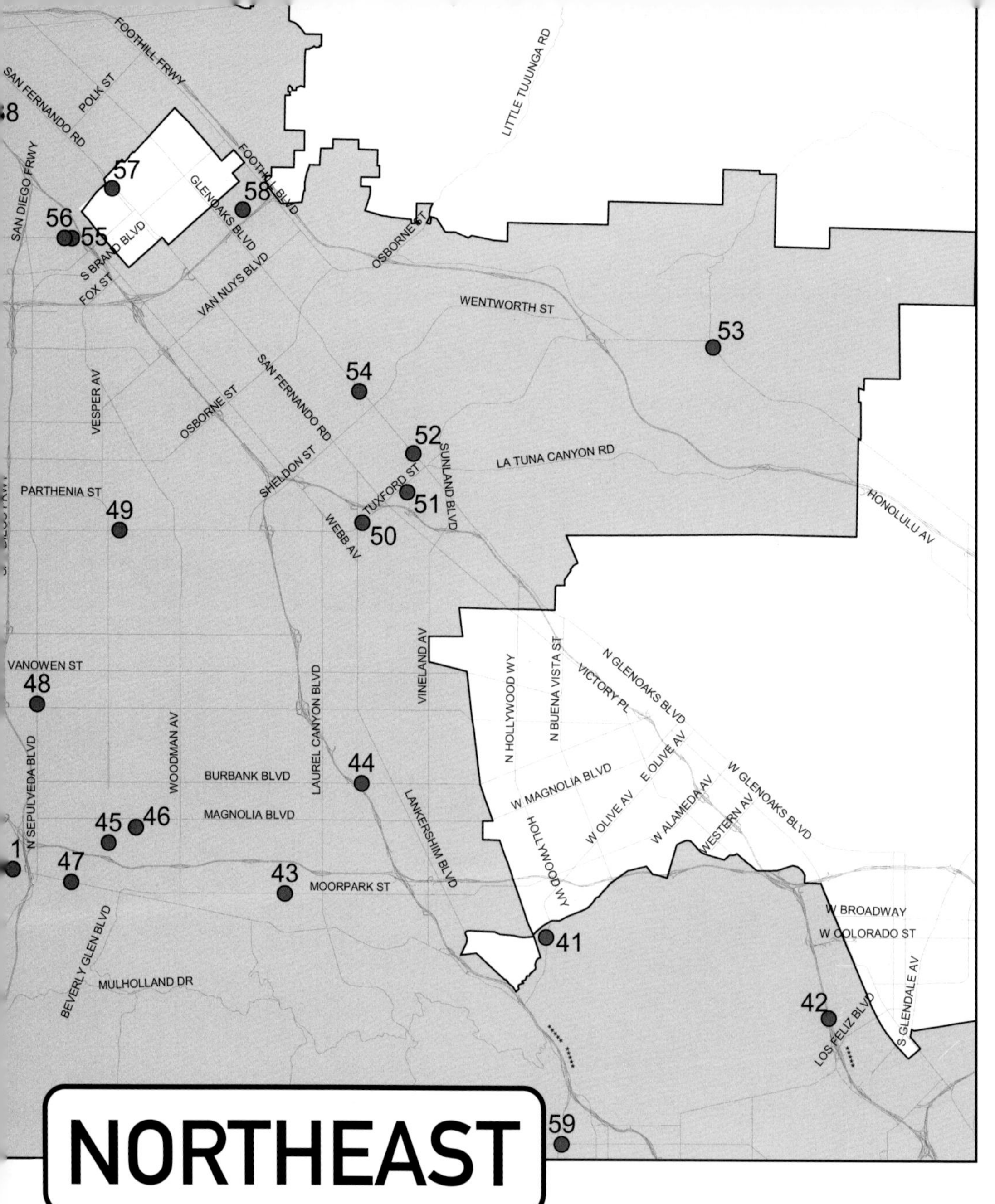

NORTHEAST

39
SAN FERNA
38
SAN DIEGO FRWY
37
36
RINALDI ST
SAN FERNANDO MISSION BLVD
SANTA SUSANA PASS RD
CHATSWORTH ST
15
12
35
DEVONSHIRE ST
RESEDA BLVD
13
14
ZELZAH AV
BALBOA BLVD
34
18
11
PLUMMER ST
32
PLUMMER ST
16
PLUMMER ST
33
17
NORDHOFF ST
10
CANOGA AV
DE SOTO AV
SAN DIEGO FRWY
PARTI
31
30
ROSCOE BLVD
19
9
8
WOODLEY AV
SATICOY ST
7
SHERMAN WY
21
SHERMAN WY
5
6
4
FALLBROOK AV
TOPANGA CANYON BLVD
WINNETKA AV
TAMPA AV
WHITE OAK AV
HAYVENHURST AV
VANOWE
29
PLATT AV
23
VICTORY BLVD
48
VALLEY CIRCLE BLVD
22
OXNARD ST
25
27
24
N SEPULVEDA BLVD
28
26
VENTURA BLVD
3
2
1
MULHOLLAND DR
MULHOLLAND HWY

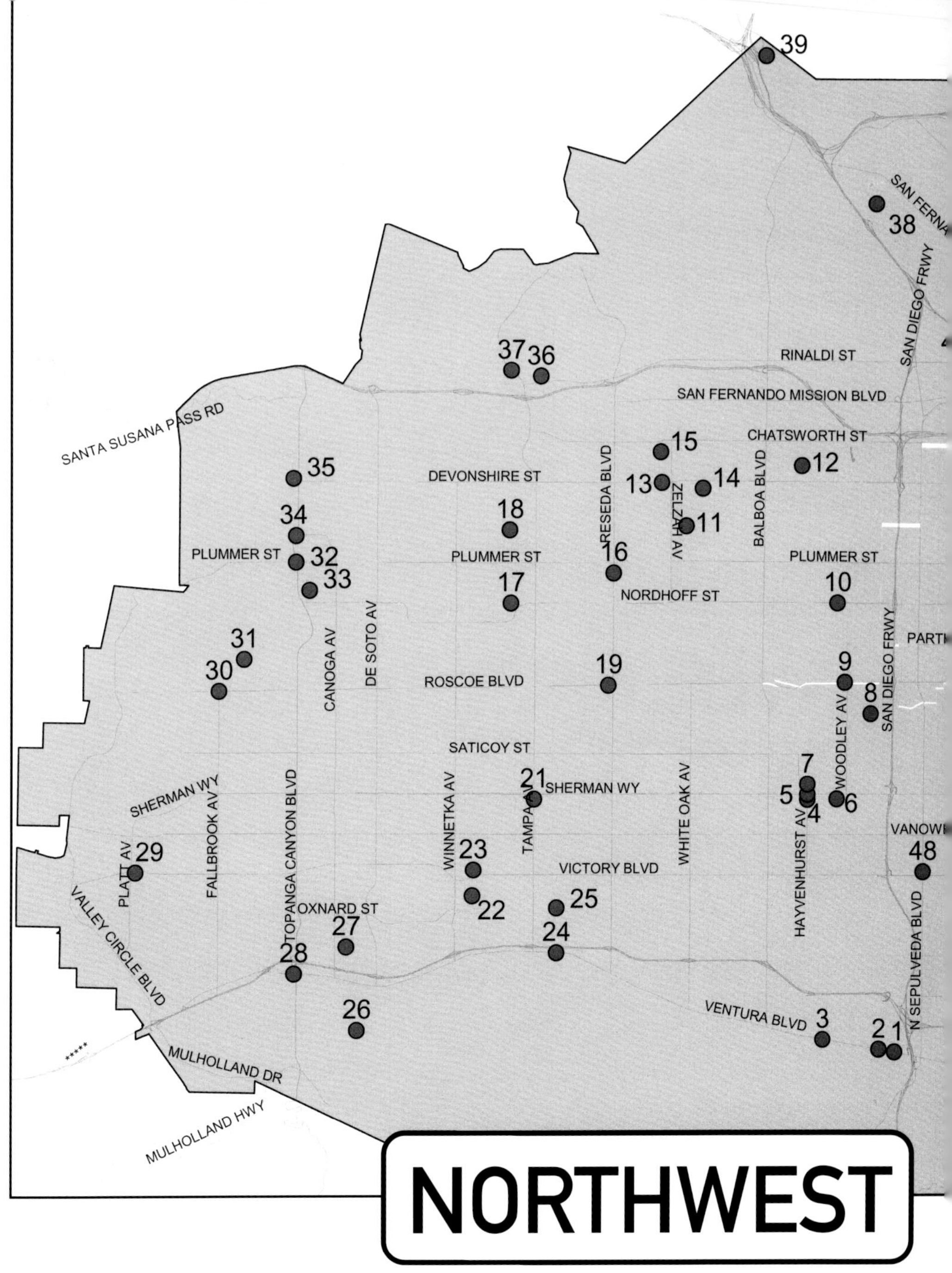

NORTHWEST

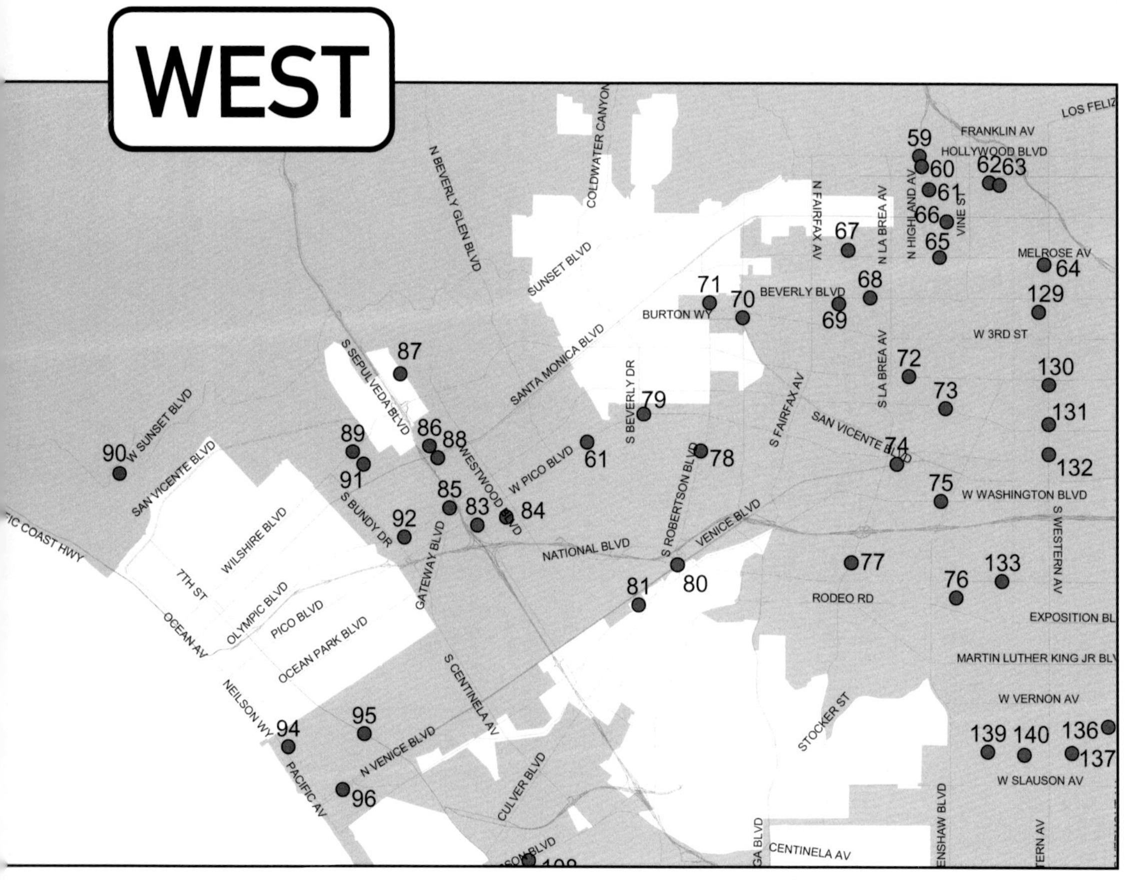

WEST
FRANKLIN AV
HOLLYWOOD BLVD
N BEVERLY GLEN BLVD
COLDWATER CANYON
SUNSET BLVD
N FAIRFAX AV
N LA BREA AV
N HIGHLAND AV
VINE ST
MELROSE AV
BEVERLY BLVD
BURTON WY
W 3RD ST
SANTA MONICA BLVD
S SEPULVEDA BLVD
S BEVERLY DR
S FAIRFAX AV
S LA BREA AV
SAN VICENTE BLVD
W SUNSET BLVD
SAN VICENTE BLVD
WESTWOOD BLVD
W PICO BLVD
S ROBERTSON BLVD
W WASHINGTON BLVD
S WESTERN AV
S BUNDY DR
GATEWAY BLVD
WILSHIRE BLVD
NATIONAL BLVD
VENICE BLVD
7TH ST
OLYMPIC BLVD
PICO BLVD
OCEAN PARK BLVD
OCEAN AV
RODEO RD
EXPOSITION BL
MARTIN LUTHER KING JR BL
W VERNON AV
NEILSON WY
S CENTINELA AV
STOCKER ST
N VENICE BLVD
PACIFIC AV
CULVER BLVD
W SLAUSON AV
CENTINELA AV
59
60
61
62
63
66
65
67
64
68
71
70
69
129
87
72
130
73
79
131
89
86
88
61
78
74
90
132
91
75
85
83
84
92
77
80
133
76
81
95
94
139
140
136
137
96

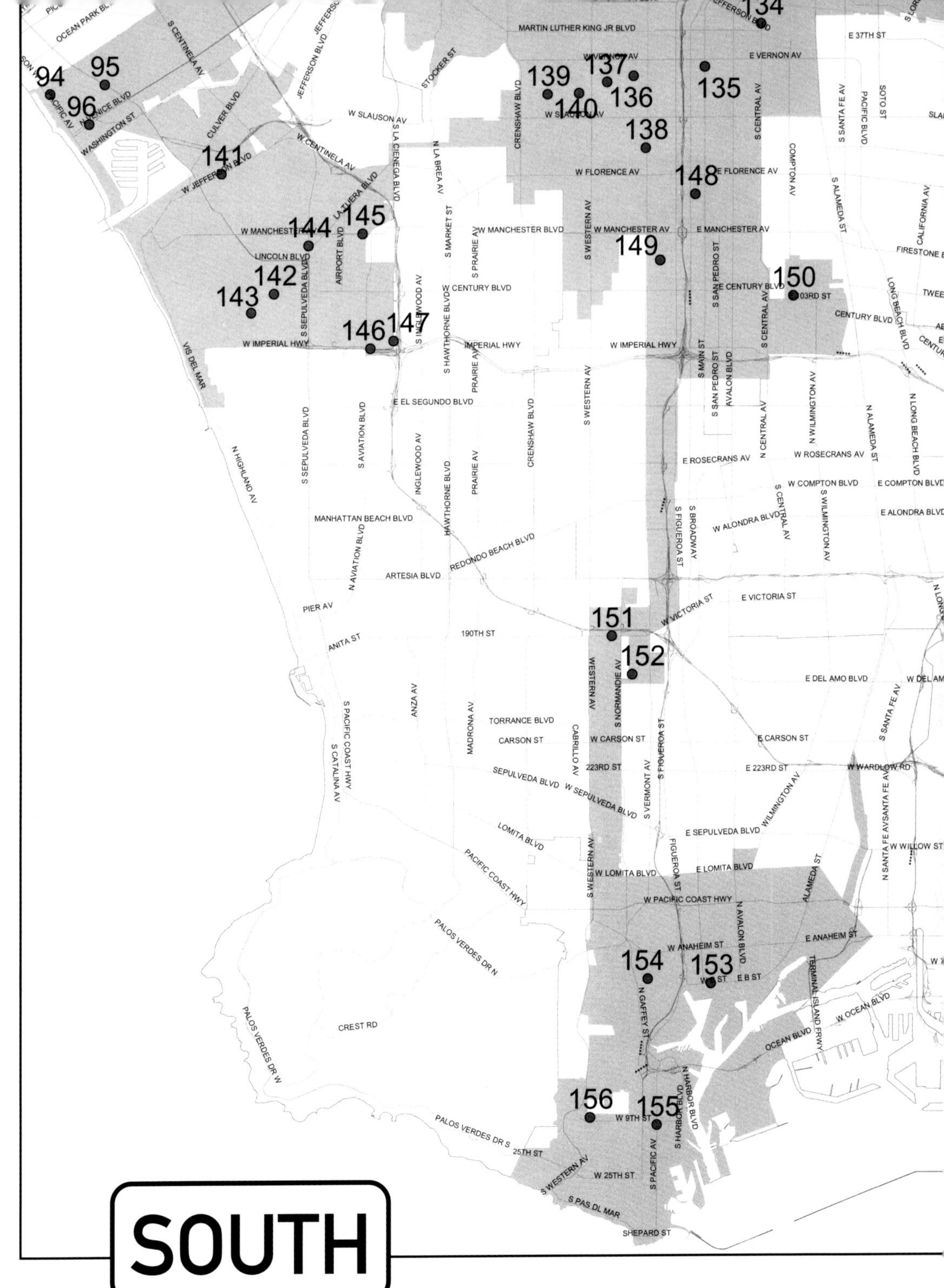

SOUTH

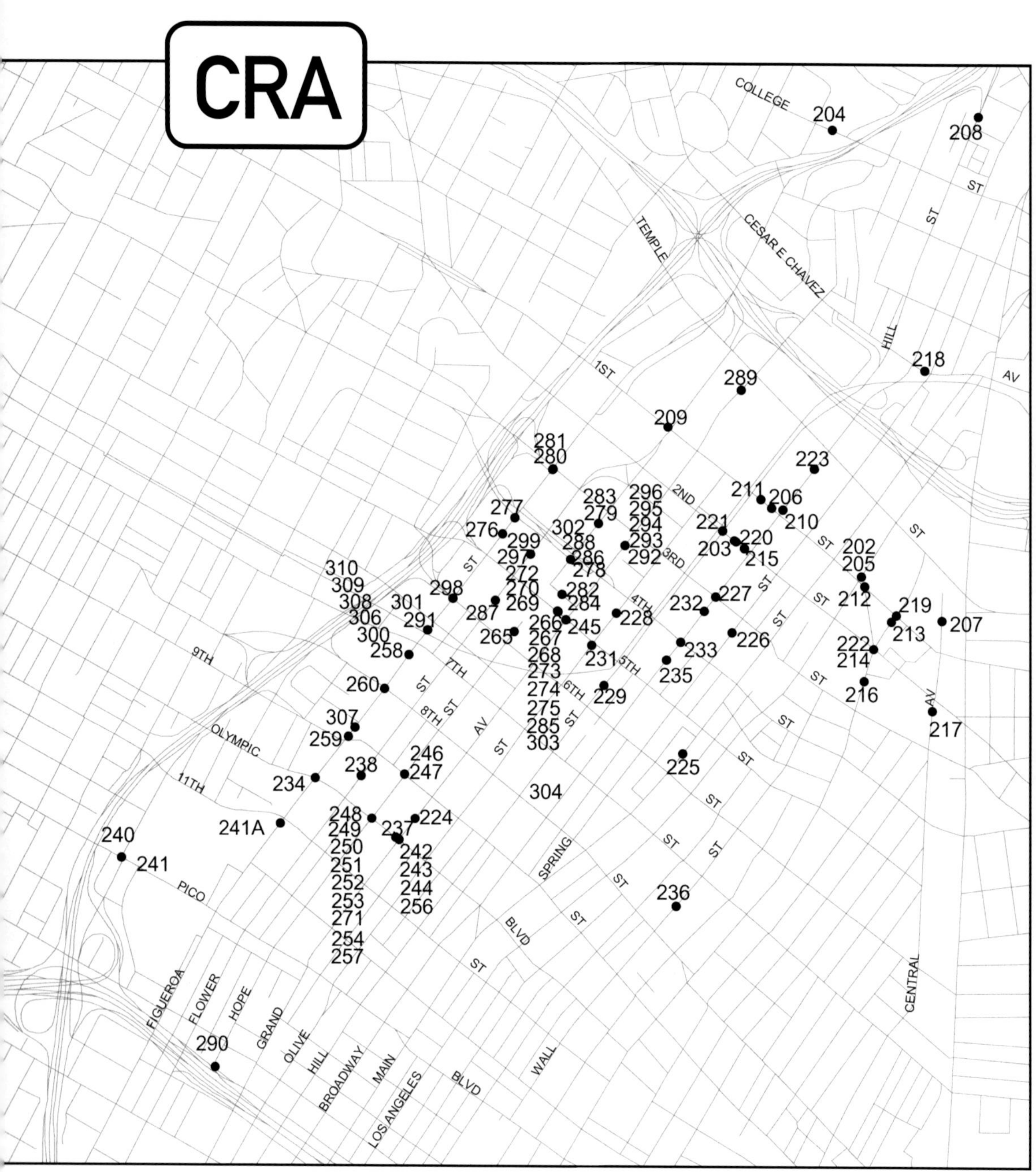
CRA
COLLEGE
TEMPLE
CESAR E CHAVEZ
HILL
1ST
2ND
3RD
4TH
5TH
6TH
7TH
8TH
9TH
OLYMPIC
11TH
PICO
FIGUEROA
FLOWER
HOPE
GRAND
OLIVE
HILL
BROADWAY
MAIN
LOS ANGELES
BLVD
WALL
SPRING
CENTRAL
AV
ST

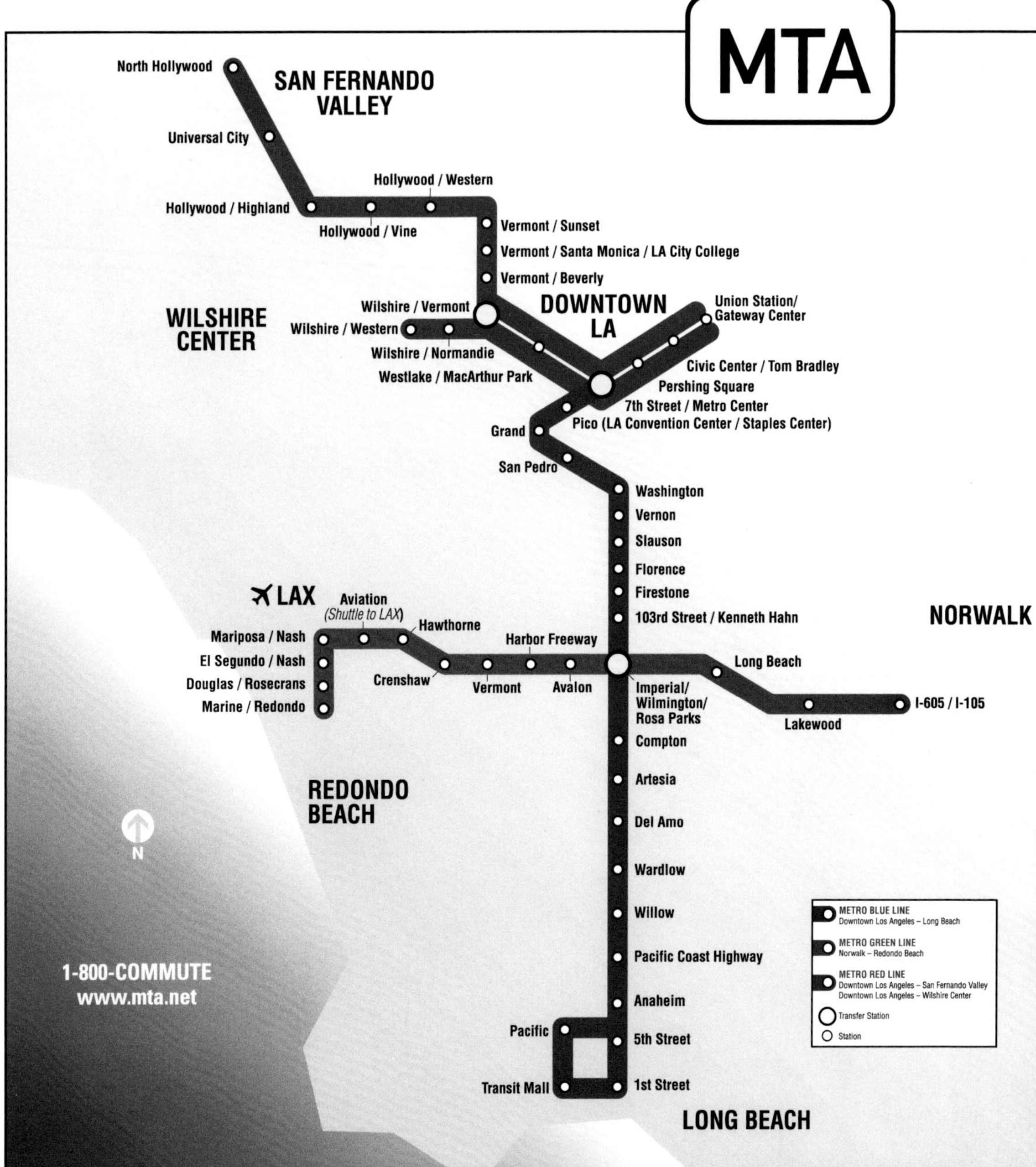
MTA
North Hollywood
SAN FERNANDO VALLEY
Universal City
Hollywood / Western
Hollywood / Highland
Hollywood / Vine
Vermont / Sunset
Vermont / Santa Monica / LA City College
Vermont / Beverly
WILSHIRE CENTER
Wilshire / Vermont
Wilshire / Western
Wilshire / Normandie
Westlake / MacArthur Park
DOWNTOWN LA
Union Station/ Gateway Center
Civic Center / Tom Bradley
Pershing Square
7th Street / Metro Center
Pico (LA Convention Center / Staples Center)
Grand
San Pedro
Washington
Vernon
Slauson
Florence
Firestone
103rd Street / Kenneth Hahn
NORWALK
LAX
Aviation
(Shuttle to LAX)
Hawthorne
Harbor Freeway
Mariposa / Nash
El Segundo / Nash
Douglas / Rosecrans
Marine / Redondo
Crenshaw
Vermont
Avalon
Long Beach
Imperial/ Wilmington/ Rosa Parks
I-605 / I-105
Lakewood
Compton
REDONDO BEACH
Artesia
Del Amo
Wardlow
Willow
Pacific Coast Highway
Anaheim
Pacific
5th Street
Transit Mall
1st Street
LONG BEACH
N
1-800-COMMUTE
www.mta.net
METRO BLUE LINE
Downtown Los Angeles – Long Beach
METRO GREEN LINE
Norwalk – Redondo Beach
METRO RED LINE
Downtown Los Angeles – San Fernando Valley
Downtown Los Angeles – Wilshire Center
Transfer Station
Station

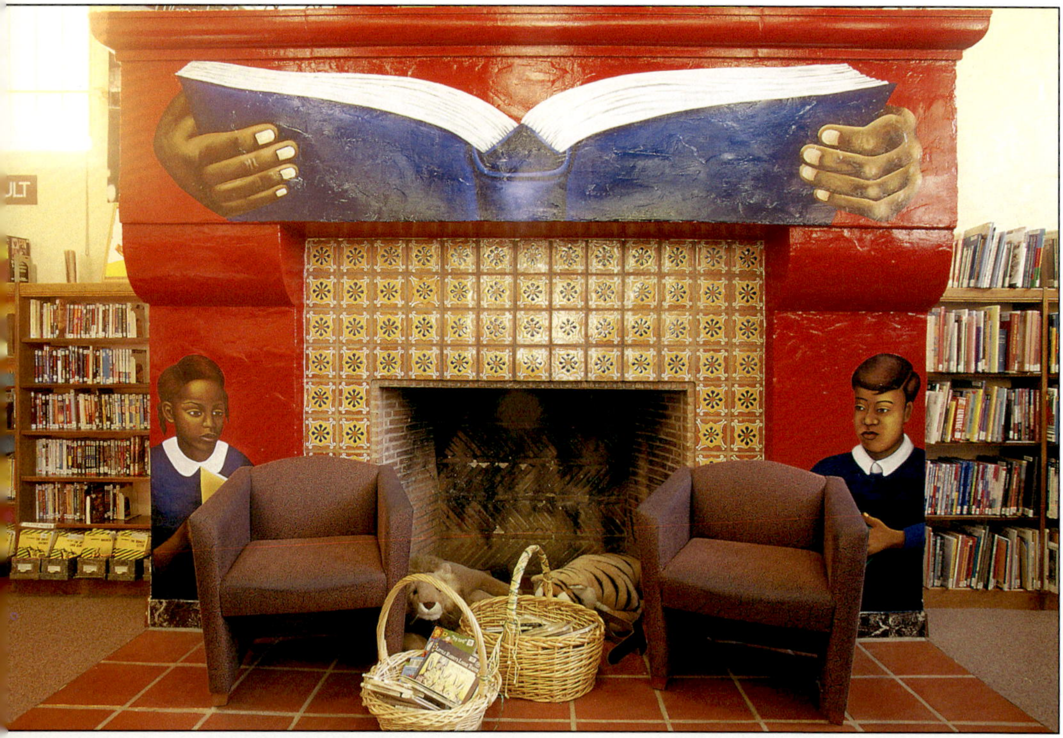

139] ANGELES MESA LIBRARY

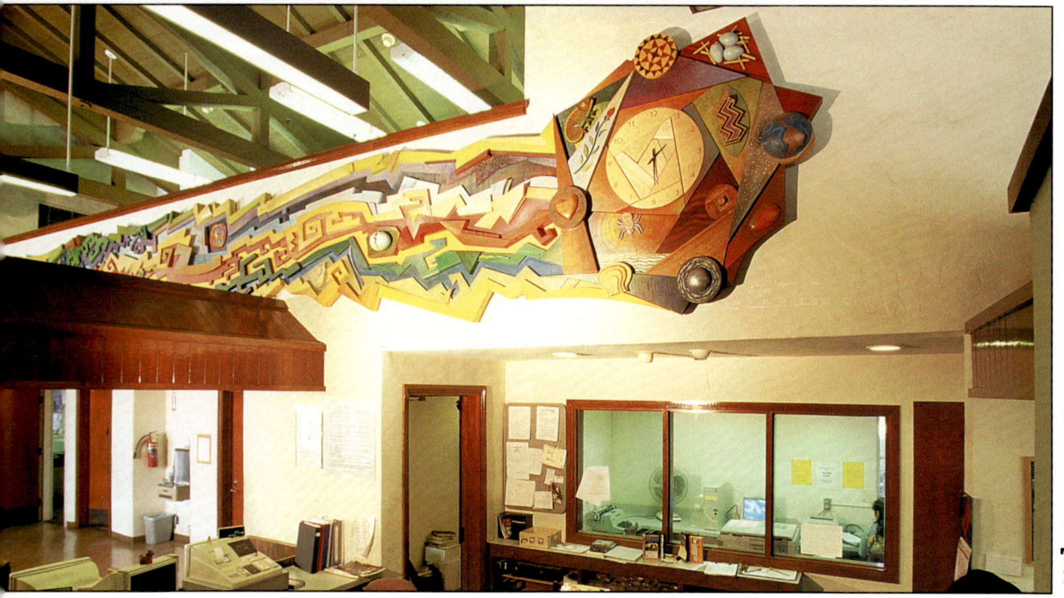

101] MALABAR LIBRARY

136] VERMONT SQUARE LIBRARY

10] MID-VALLEY LIBRARY

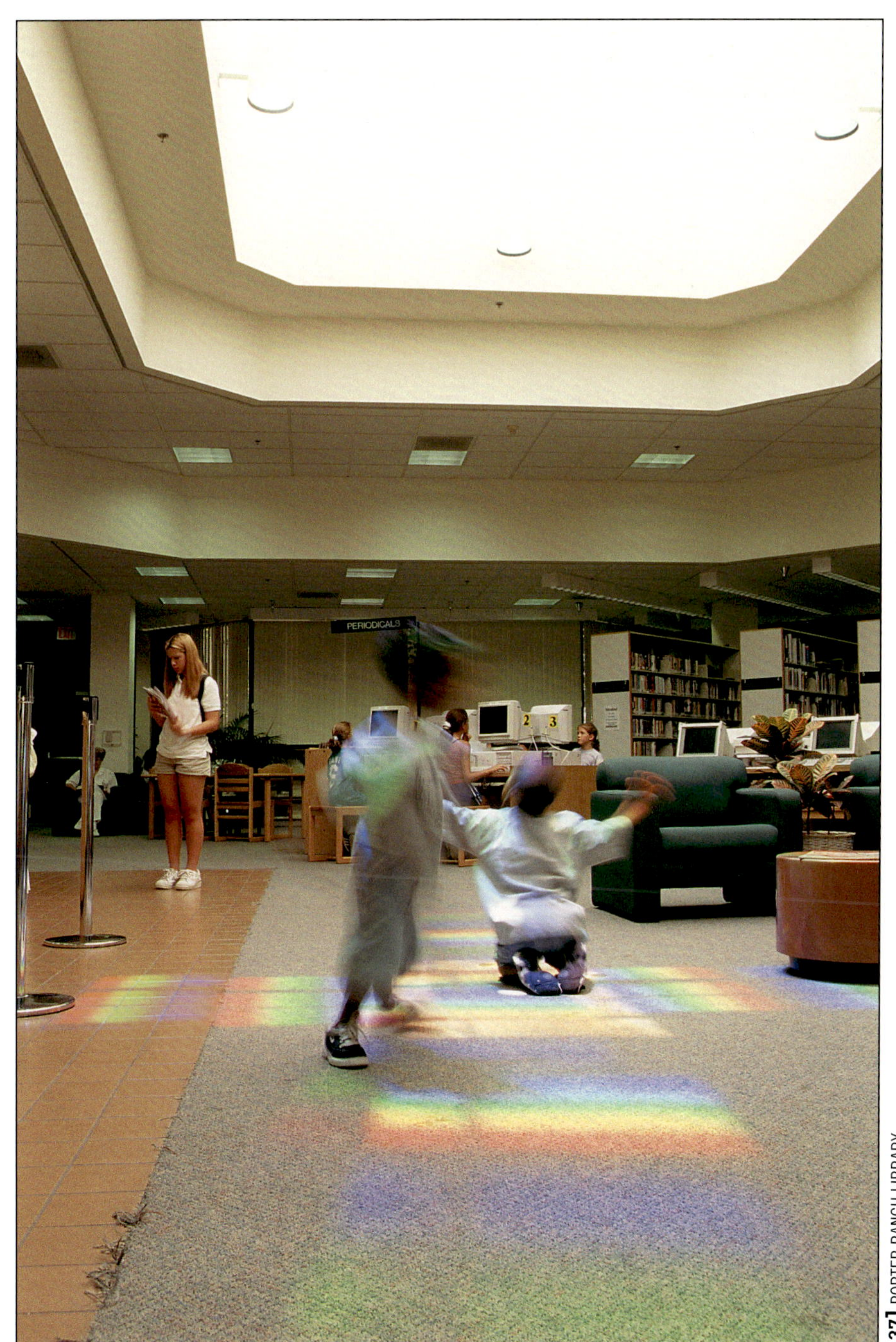

37] PORTER RANCH LIBRARY

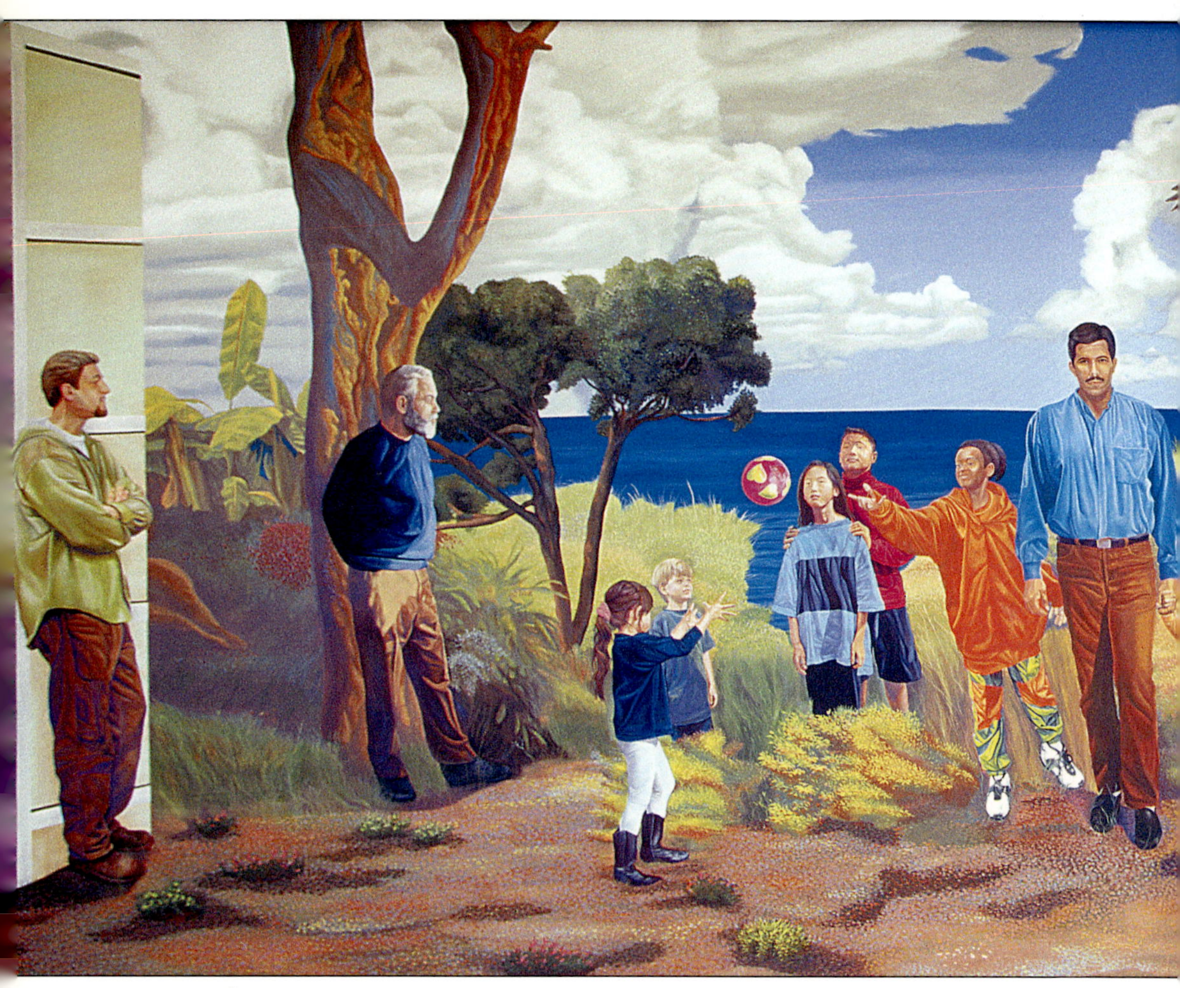

124] ST. VINCENT MEDICAL CENTER

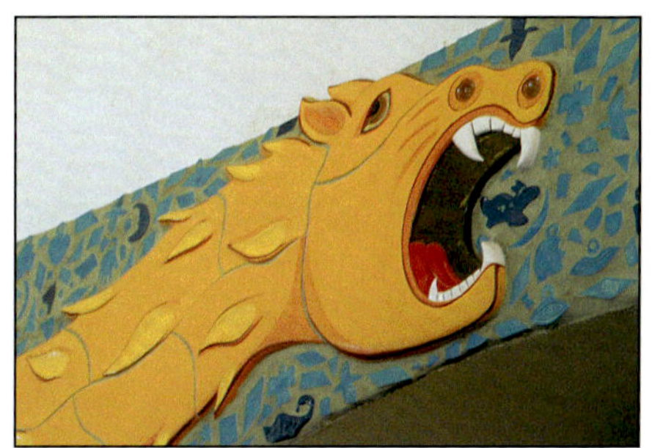

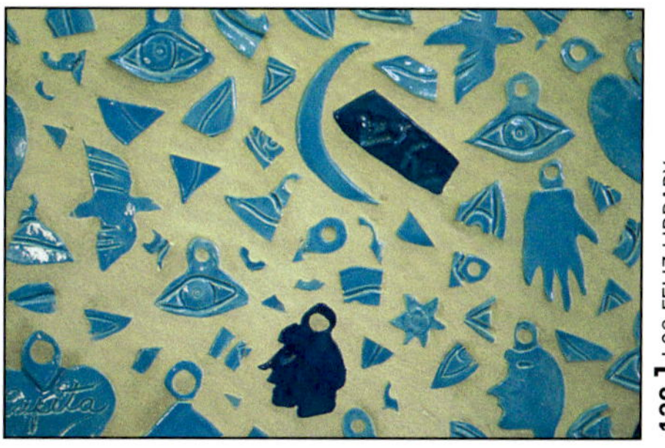

128] LOS FELIZ LIBRARY

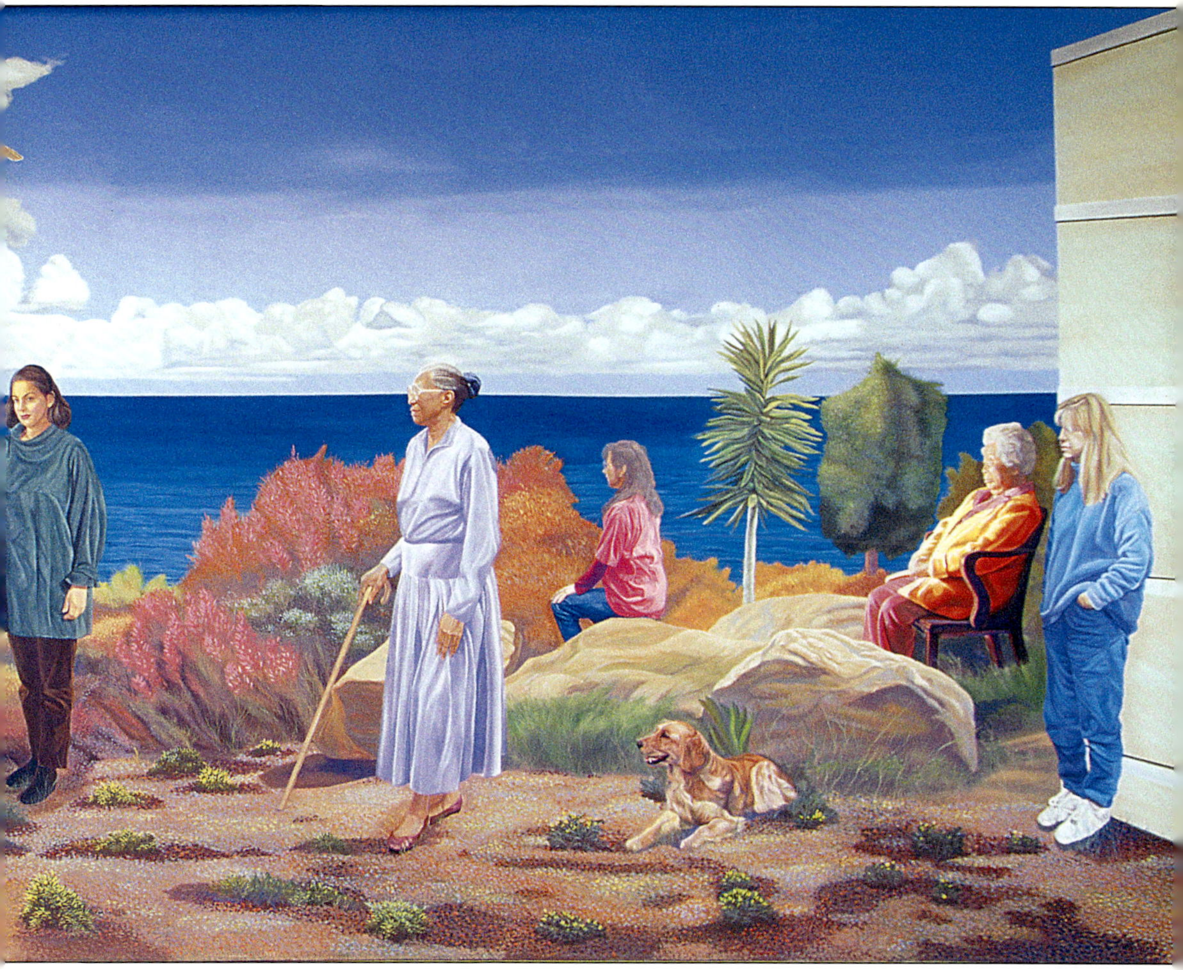

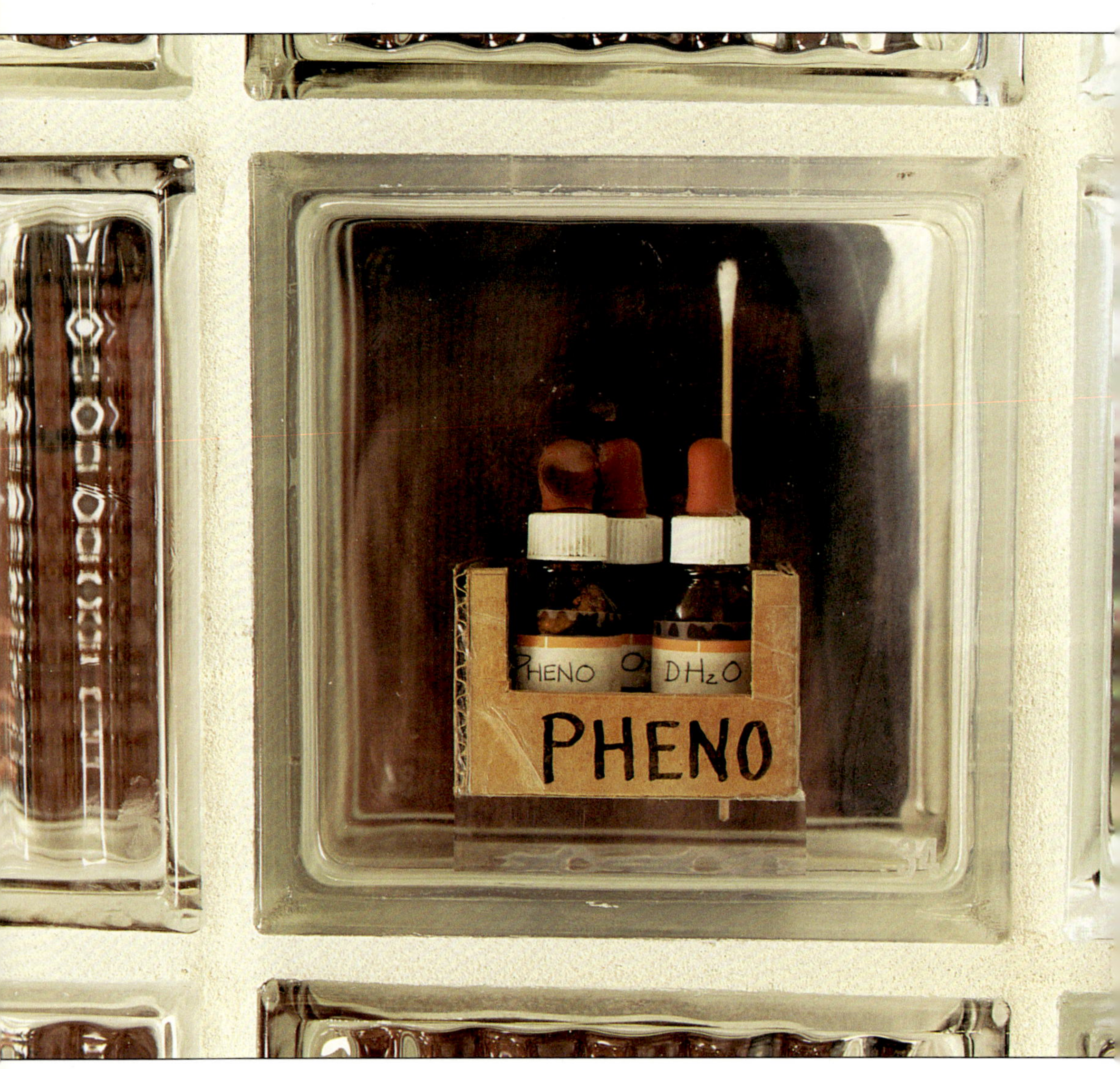
PHENO
DH2O
PHENO

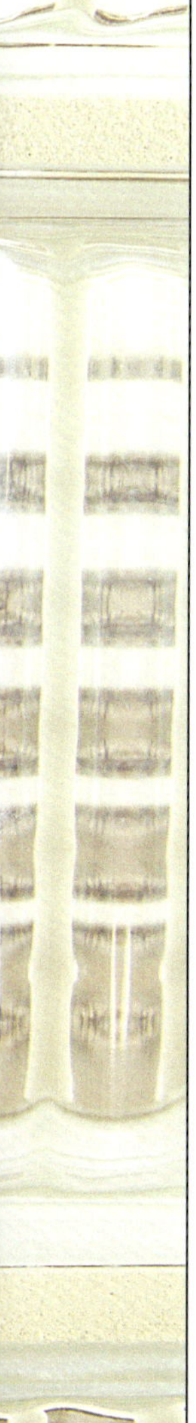

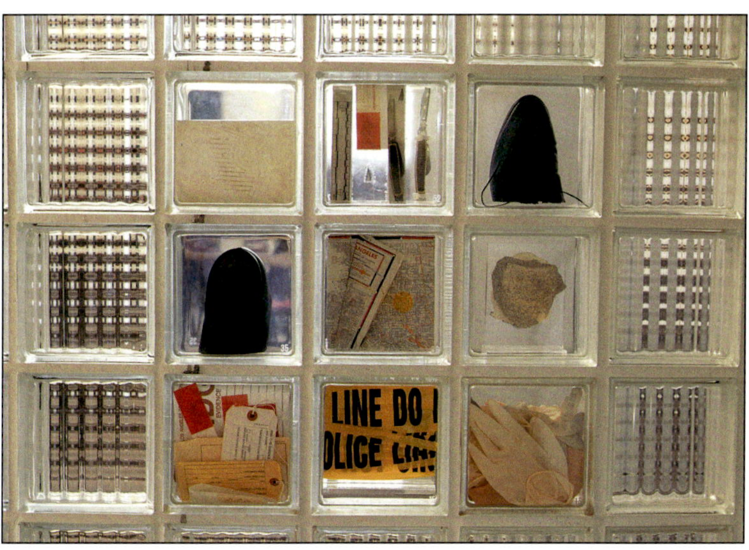

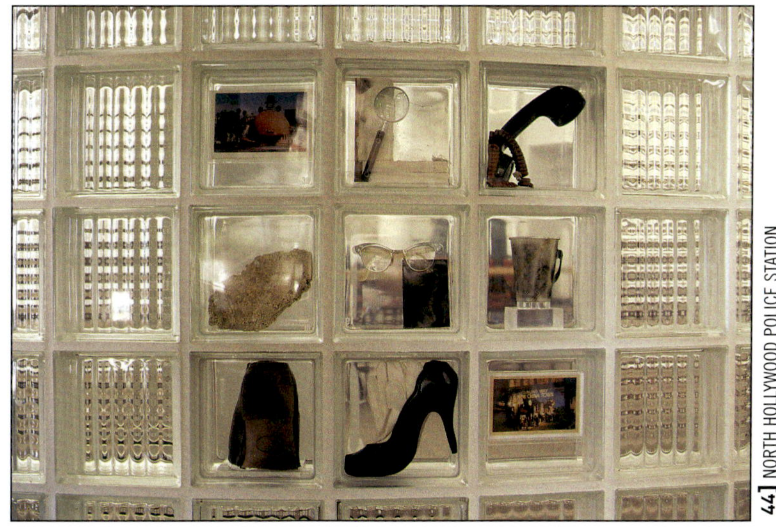

44] NORTH HOLLYWOOD POLICE STATION

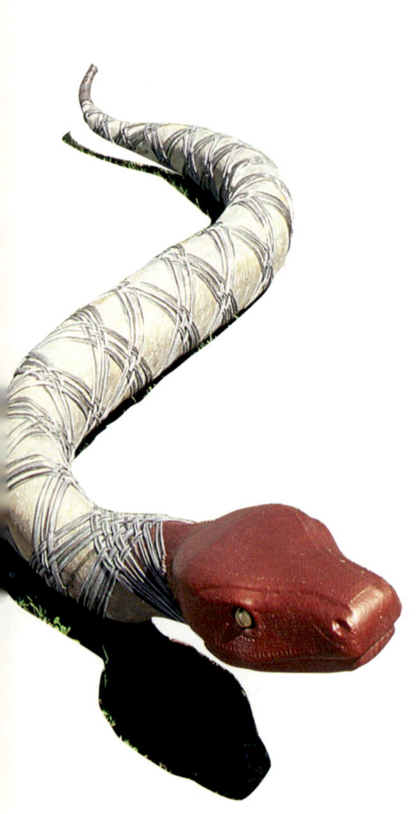

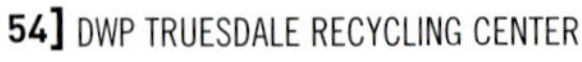
54] DWP TRUESDALE RECYCLING CENTER

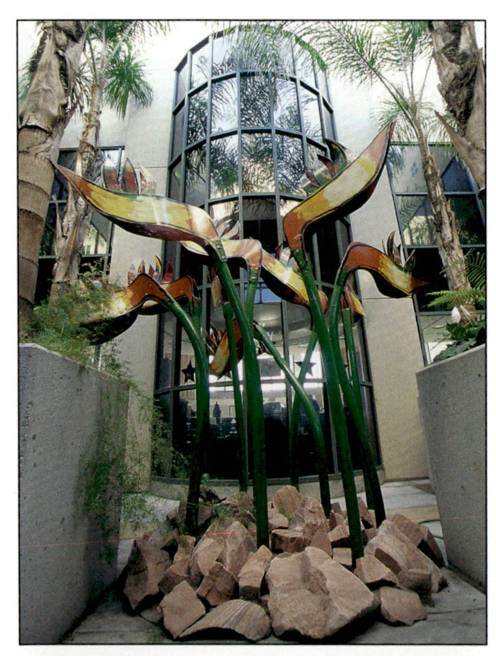

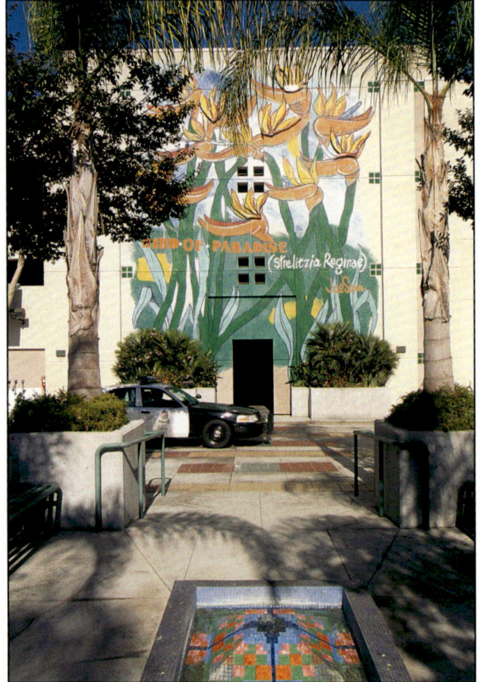

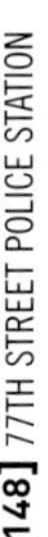
148] 77TH STREET POLICE STATION

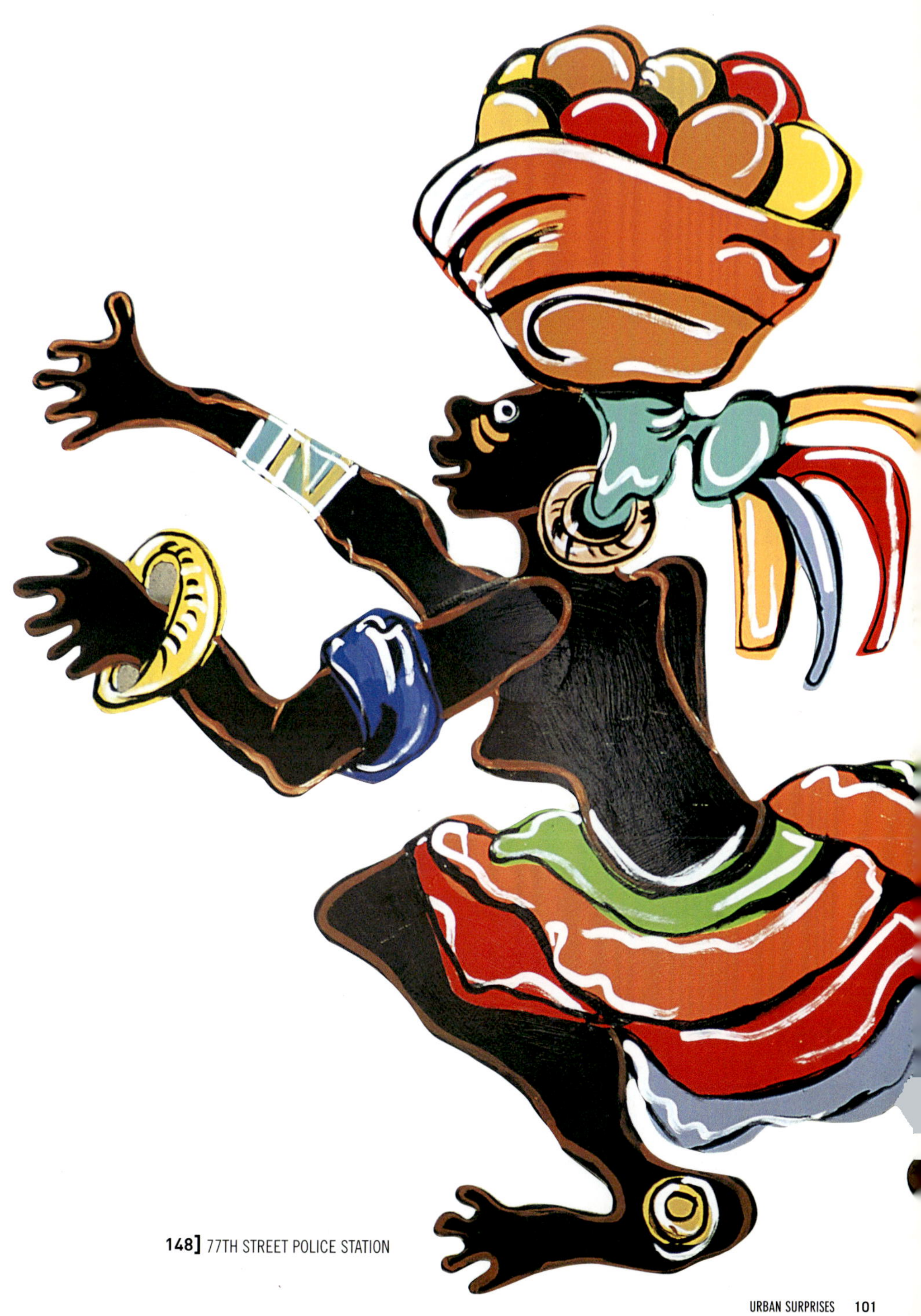

148] 77TH STREET POLICE STATION

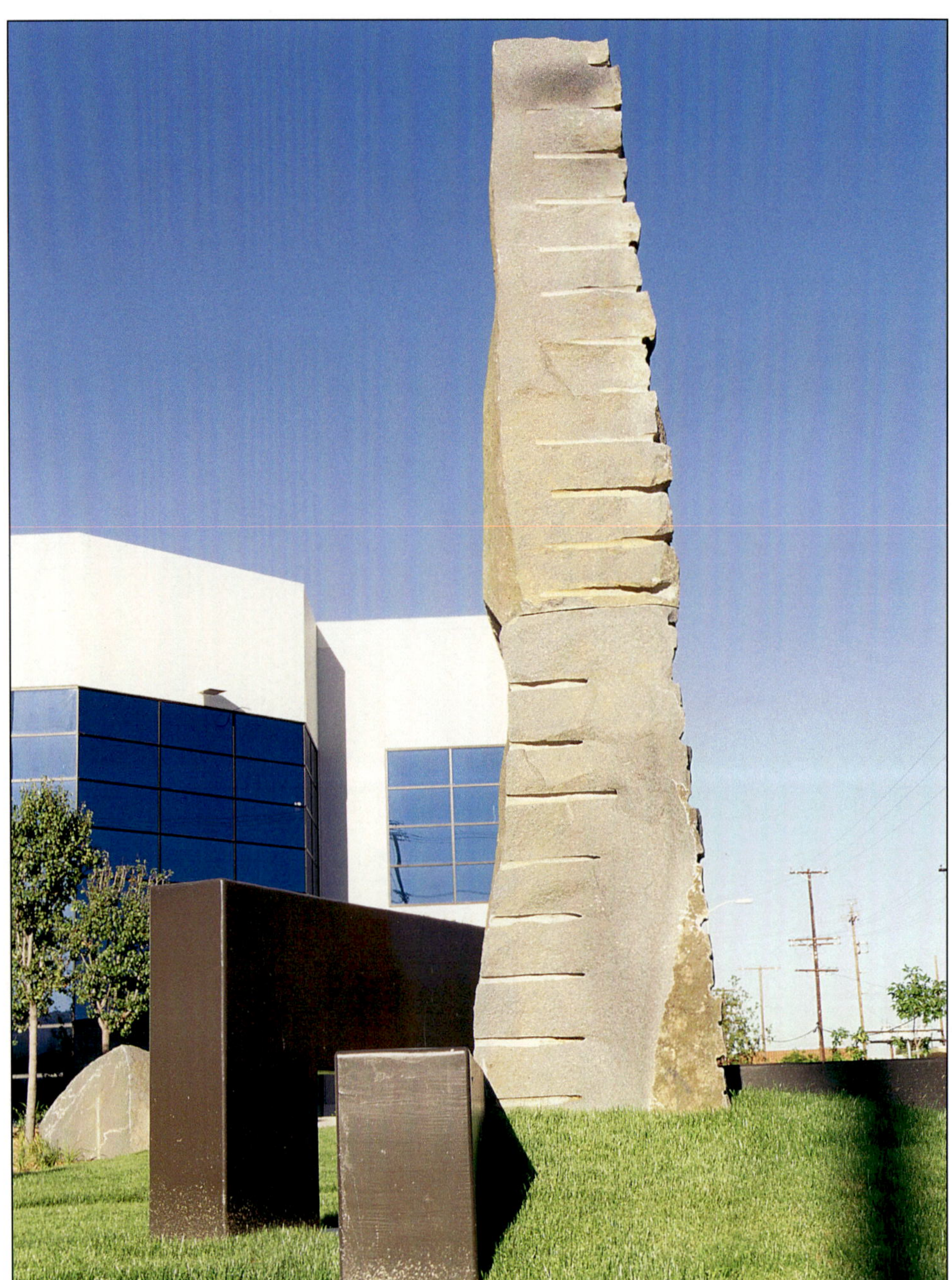

8] THE LEWIS COMPANY

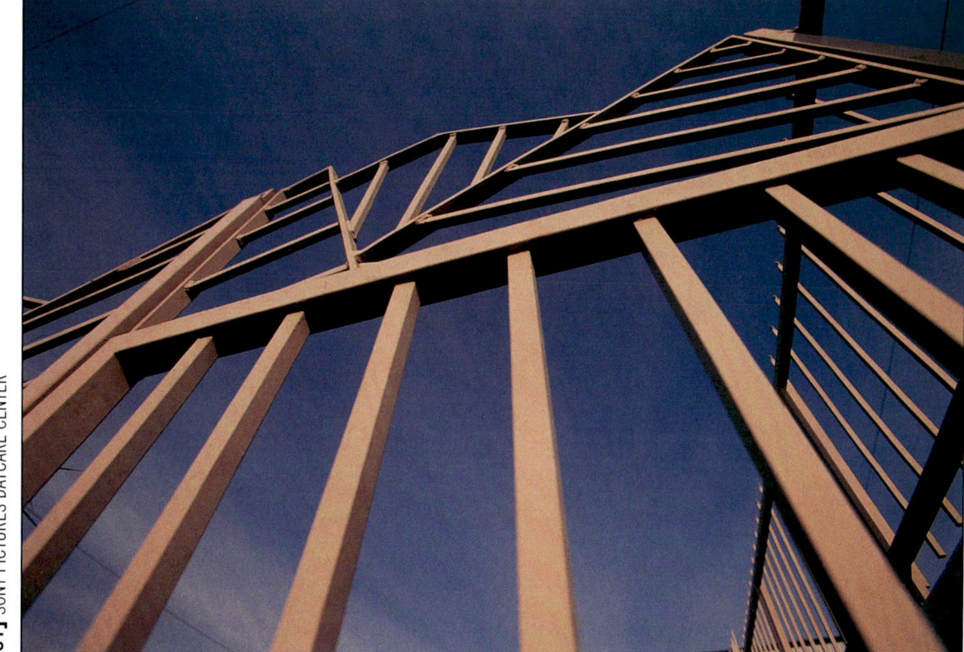

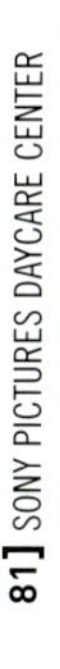

81] SONY PICTURES DAYCARE CENTER

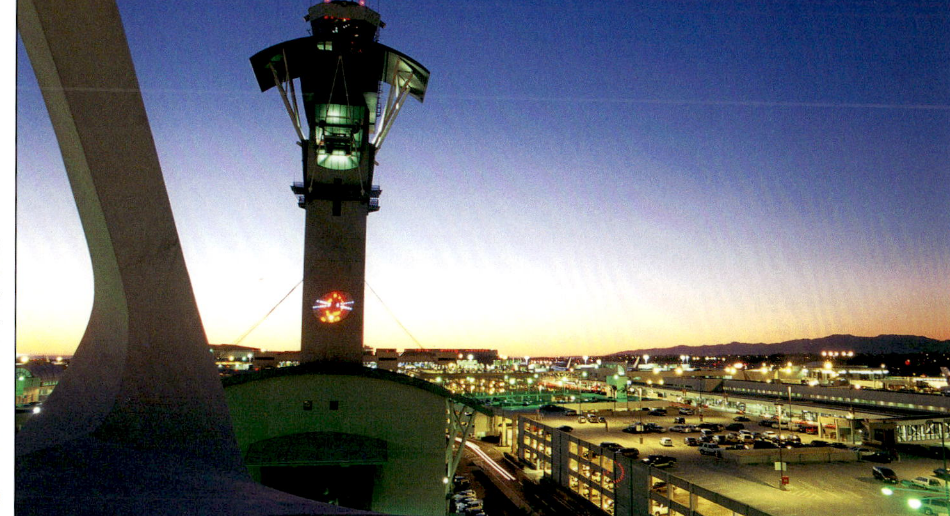

142] AIR TRAFFIC CONTROL (FAA) AT LAX

LIST OF SPONSORS

CULTURAL AFFAIRS ARTS PROGRAMS SPONSORS

658 VENICE LTD. Provided storage space for LA arts organizations
ADVANCE PAPER BOX CO. Supporter Performing Tree at W/59th St. School
ALL ABOARD MINI-STORAGE Provided storage space for arts organizations
AMERICAN INTERCONTINENTAL UNIVERSITY Supported high school Art and Design program and exhibition
ARBA GROUP (THE LAUREL CENTER GROUP) Collaborated with CBS to provide funds for media arts center at local school
AROMA SPOREX Supported arts programming on video sign display
AROMA SPOREX Provided free space for artists and arts organizations on the program of an 800 square foot video display
AVIA DEV. CORP. Restored historic building
BEN REININGER Supported African Marketplace/Cultural fair
BRINKER RESTAURANT COPORATION Created program of opera singers in restaurant
BUY LINES Provided in kind services for Evans Adult School
CABLE VISION INDUSTRIES Provided production and editing services for artist Rohini Tallala's "Asphalt Indian"
CBS Provided studios for rehearsals and classes for Jazz Tap Ensemble and collaborated with Arba development to provide funds for media arts center in local school.
CENTURY NATIONAL INSURANCE Provided office space for Mozart Orchestra
CENTURY WEST BMW Sponsored animation art in classroom program in local area schools
CERELL CO. Provided public relations services for Greek Theater/ Bilingual Foundation for Arts
CLMC / HAL NORRIS Provided warehouse space for Cornerstone Theater
COVENANT HOUSE Sponsored art classes at Covenant House
DAVID OVED Sponsored an arts exchange between Keshet Chaim Dance Ensemble and the Inbal Dance Theatre from Israel for a series of workshops, rehearsals, and performances
DUCKHORN PROPERTIES Sponsored "Music in the Schools Program" which supports several different music education programs.
DYNAMIC BUILDERS Sponsored variety of art and music programs in local schools, including the upsARTS program.
EL PROYECTO DEL BARRIO Sponsored exhibit and folklorico performance
EL WALL PARTNERSHIP Provided office space for The Brotherhood Through the Arts Foundation
EXTRA SPACE MANAGEMENT Provided storage space to arts organizations
FISCH PROPERTIES Provided in kind services for The Brotherhood for the Arts Foundation
FULL GOSPEL LA CHURCH Sponsored cultural programming with Korean American Youth Choir & Korean Philharmonic Orchestra
GEMINI INDUSTRIES Provided in kind services for Creative Response
GO ENTERPRISES Sponsored three festival events with Hispanic artists
GREAT WESTERN PROPERTY CO. Provided free rent for Road Theatre Co.
HAZAMA CORP. Sponsored film festival funding and space
HEBREW UNION COLLEGE Provided cultural Programming and various art pieces
HILLCREST CHRISTIAN SCHOOL Funded Kids in Motion, an after school art appreciation program for students in K-12
HOLLYWOOD CENTER STUDIO Provided in kind services for Koreatown Blues
HOME DEPOT USA Donated money to Valley Cultural Center Trust Fund for music in the park series
HOME DEPOT USA Sponsored productions in coordination with the Assistance League of Southern California
HOME DEPOT USA Sponsored Alternative Routes for the Woodworking Bus program at three Van Nuys elementary schools
HOME DEPOT USA Sponsored Angels Gate for their Artist in Classroom program allowing the program to extended to three more schools
HOME DEPOT USA Sponsored KYDS's (Keep Youth Doing Something) Community Mural and Playhouse projects
ILAN BENDER Provided sculpture by Armenyan Tsolak
JONATHAN COOKLER Provided space for Heartworld
KABC RADIO Provided airtime for Los Angeles Cultural Affairs events
KANE CONSTRUCTION Provided equipment and material for renovation of El Portal Theatre for Actor's Alley
KLST PARTNERSHIP Provided in-kind storage space to LA arts organizations
LA COLISEUM Sponsored historic preservation in coliseum
LA CURACAO Sponsored series of cultural performances
LA TIMES DISTRIBUTION BLDG. Sponsored outreach program with the Museum of Contemporary Art
LAINER INVESTMENTS Provided funding to North Valley Family Festival Keshet Chaim Dance Co
LAINER INVESTMENTS Provided funds to Inner City Film Makers for professional filmmaking classes in two local LAUSD high schools
LAINER INVESTMENTS Provided funds to Guild Opera Company to sponsor two performances of "Alice in Wonderland" at twelve

LAUSD elementary schools
LEONARD FISCH Brotherhood Through the Arts Foundation
LOS ANGELES EXPORT TERMINAL INC. Contribution to Warner Grand Theatre restoration
LOS ANGELES WORLD AIRPORT Sponsored kinetic light display program for the LAX Gateway Pylons Project
LOWE DEVELOPMENT LA Mexican Dance Aca, 1st Impressions, LA Choreographer & Dancer and contributed space to Loretta Livingston & Dancers
LUCKY STORES Donated to African Market Place
MACLEOD PARTNERSHIP Historic renovation satisfied requirement
MAGIC JOHNSON THEATERS Created an artwork and film series celebrating the professional career of Magic Johnson
MANN THEATRES Provided free on screen advertising for Non Profit Arts Organizations
MIKE BUJKO Sponsored exhibit art and performance by Fusion Melange Teamsters
MILAN WEISS Provided services for Hancock Park Civic Light Opera
MORT ALLEN Provided subsidized rent for theater group
OSAKA SANGYO UNIV. LA Sponsored cultural programming
PACIFIC THEATRES CORP Collaborated with International Documentary Association on outreach program with Wonder for Reading, a media education in elementary school libraries
PARAMOUNT PICTURES Provided space and support for CA Youth Theatre
PEP BOYS Sponsored series of art programs including Los Angeles Unified School District Facilities Enhancement project.
PHILLIPS PLYWOOD Donated to Materials for the Arts
PTA Sponsored various programs including scholarships for music
PUBLIC STORAGE INC Provided community art program and provided storage space for a variety of organizations
REGINALD ARNOLD Provided services for California Afro-American Museum
ROCKWELL INTERNATIONAL Cultural Programming-KCET Bella Lewitsky Dance Foundation, Bilingual for Arts, LA Chamber Symphony Society, Guild Opera Co, California Museum, Foundation of LA, KUSC-FM, Southwest Museum
ROMAN CATHOLIC ARCHBISHOP OF LOS ANGELES Provided dance and music events at their site
ROSCOE DEVELOPMENT COMPANY Contribution to Keshet Chaim Dance Ensemble for Milken High School dance and education program
S & S PARTNERSHIP Sponsored art competition and event with local Latino/Chicano/Central American artists
SALVATION ARMY Provided workshops, materials and work space to residents and others
SANTA MONICA/BELOIT PTSHP./CLOVERLEAF Sponsored photographic exhibition onsite
SAWTELLE SELF STORAGE Provided storage space for arts organizations
SCOTT SEOL Provided in kind services for Korean American Youth Choir
SHERMAN OAKS FASHION SQUARE Sponsored a series of performances and exhibits
SIMPSON, JOHN Provided theater space for LA Cultural Theatre
SINAGUA PLAZA ASSOCIATES Sponsored Angels Gate Cultural Center's Artist in Classroom Program for programming in two schools
SO CAL INSTITUTE OF ARCHITECTURE Sponsored free lecture series
SUNSHINE DISTRIBUTION LP HARBOR GATEWAY Provided art space and art programming for Wilmington Boys & Girls Club
TBWA/CHIAT/DAY Sponsored the Light-Bringer Project for the Mentorship Program and the Chalk-In event in conjunction with LAUSD
TEMPLE ADAT ARU EL Provided music events, an annual youth play, and adult art classes at their site
TERRY GREENE Provided cultural programming by tenant Junior Philharmonic Orchestra
TEXACO Provided arts grants which were distributed to organizations to support school arts programs
TISHMAN WARNER CENTER Sponsored the Boys Scouts of America for their "Careers in Culture" Program in conjunction with the fine arts department at Cal State University Northridge. Funding was also given to sponsor The Madrid Theatre for local arts programming.
TWENTIETH CENTURY FOX FILM CORPORATION Sponsored storytelling program in schools using murals and films
VENICE FAMILY CLINIC Sponsored Venice "Art Walk"
VERNON MAIN PHARMACY Provided printing services for the California African-American Museum
WARNER CENTER Hired art instructors for day care center
WESTCHESTER FAMILY YMCA Sponsored dance classes
WEST HILLS CORPORATE VILLAGE Provided funds to the Cal State University Northridge/LAUSD Arts Partnership for classes at schools

LIST OF CONTRIBUTORS

COMPANIES AND INDIVIDUALS WHO CONTRIBUTED TO THE CULTURAL AFFAIRS ARTS FUND

1000 WALL ST. ASSOCIATES
11105 LA CIENEGA PROPERTIES
2080 BUNDY LLC
3M PHARMACEUTICALS
8000 SUNSET LTD.
A.C. PRODUCTION
ADAMS WEST PARTNERSHIP
AJIT DEVELOPMENT
ALBERT ELKOUBY
ALPHA THERAPEUTIC CORPORATION
AMB INSTITUTIONAL REALTY
AMC INC.
AMIR POURZANJANI
ANHEUSER-BUSCH
ANTONIO DELGADO
ARKENBERG, FRED & LINDA
ARNOLD CARLSON
ARNOLD SCHWARZENEGGER
AVIA DEVELOPMENT GROUP
AVIATION ASSOCIATION
B.B WORLD CORPORATION
BARTH SELMA
BAXTER HEALTHCARE
BAY SUITES PARTNERS
BC PROPERTIES
BEHROOZ
BEST BUY
BHOJAK TRILOK
BIGNAL PRODUCTS
BINNY FASHIN
BLUE BALL ENTERPRISES
BUILDING MANAGEMENT SERVICES
BUNDY ASSOCIATES INC.
BURNS, FRITZ B FOUNDATION
CAL-ASIA PROPERTY DEVELOPMENT CO.
CALIFORNIA DRIVE-IN THEATRES
CALIFORNIA FASHION INDUSTRY
CAMILLUS T. DECINES
CAROLE LITTLE
CATELLUS DEVELOPMENT
CORPORATION
CBS
CEDARS SINAI MEDICAL CENTER
CENTURY 1177 ASSOC. LLC
CHAMPION DEVELOPMENT GROUP
CHANDRA PURHIT
CHANNEL GATEWAY L.P. /J
CHARLES CO.
CHEF AMERICA
CHERNITSKY, JOSEPH
CHEVRON USA INC.
CHRIS CHEN
CIBA-GEIGY CORPORATION
CITY OF LA
CITY OF LA DEPARTMENT OF REC & PARK
CLARENCE JO SLATER
COAST FEDERAL SAVING AND LOANS
COMMUNITY BUILD INC.
CONTINENTAL GRAPHICS
COSTCO WHOLESALE CORP.
CRI-HELP, INC.
CRUISERS CAR WASH INC.
CUNNINGHAM INVESTMENTS
D.A. RAMOS
DALBY, BEN
DAN BERG DEVELOPMENT
DATA ANALYSIS INC.
DAVID AZART
DAVID DROR
DAVID FARR
DAVID SIM
DEAN ROSS
DEPARTMENT OF HARBORS
DEPARTMENT OF PUBLIC WORKS
DEPARTMENT OF WATER AND POWER
DEPT. OF AIRPORTS
DISTRIBUTION AND AUTO SERVICE
DOBBS INT'L SERVICES(B.A
DOLGIN, AARON ET AL
DON TRONSTEIN
DONGKUK INTERNATIONAL
DOWNTOWN REAL PROP ACQ, LL
DR, S. KANG
DR. ANTHONY AWAD
DR. BESHARAT
DR. DONALD HENDERSON
DR. FRED EMMANUEL
DR. RAMIN
DYNAMIC BUILDERS
E & E TRUST OF 1975
EDISON, REUBEN
EL PUEBLO COMMUNITY DEVELOPMENT
ELI HAIM
ELLIS REALTY PARTNERS
ENRIQUE ALEJO
EQUITABLE NISSEI FIGUEROA CO.
ERNESTINA GONZALES
ERP
EVELYN GOODMAN
EXTENDED STAY CA, INC.
F. KANGAVARI
F. KANGAVARI
FALLBROOK SQUARE PARTNERS
FARMER BROS. COFFEE
FEDERAL EXPRESS
FESTIVAL MANAGEMENT GROUP
FIRST BUSINESS BANK
FIRST NATIONWIDE BANK
FRAKHONDEH, ALI
FRANK RANDALL
FRESH CHOICE RESTAURANTS
GANGI BUILDERS INC.
GAS COMPANY
GATEWAY FREIGHT SERVICE INC.
GENERAL GROWTH MANAGEMENT
GEORGE & ROBERTA TORRES
GEORGE SHACKLEFORD
GILBERT AZAFRANI
GILBERT SCHNEIDER
GLUCK DEVELOPMENT CO. INC.
GOOD GUYS, THE
GOVERNMENT FUNDING CALIFORNIA
GRANADA HILLS MARKETPLACE
HAMID NOURI
HAN KOOK PLAZA INC.
HANNA BARBERA PRODUCTIONS
HARKAM INDUSTRIES
HENRY SMITH
HERB TOBMAN
HERBERT ROSTAND
HERTZ CORP., THE
HEWSON COMPANY
HOLY CROSS MEDICAL CENTER
HOME DEPOT USA
HOTEL GRANDE ASSOCIATION
HOUSING AUTHORITY OF L.A.
HOWARD HARTRY
HOWARD WIZENBERT
HOYA LENS OF AMERICA INC.
HRATCH SARKIS
HUGHES FAMILY MARKETS
I.P.D.R. ASSOC L.P.
ICE SKATING RINK
IKWHAN OH/ H K MARKET
IN-N-OUT BURGER
INTERSTATE CONSOLIDATED
IRAJ KASEUASA
ITT EDUCATIONAL SERVICE
J. SNYDER CO.
JAKE BERLMUTTER
JAMES C. SHIM
JANG BAI SAN INC.
JERRY FRIEDMAN
JOHN AMOROSA
JOHN DAVIS
JOHN S. SYMONDS ET AL

JOHNNY NELSON
K ASSOC. ET AL
K MART CORP.
K. SHAKIB
KAISER FOUNDATION HOSPITAL
KAISER PERMANENTE
KENSHI, SHINANO CORP.
KILROY REALTY L.P
KIM PHUOG JEWELRY INC.
KIM, WHA
KLABIN/SULLIVAN/BEESEN
KONOIKE MAUST CO
KOREAN YOUTH CENTER
KORNWASSER & FRIEDMAN
L.A. CITY
L.S.J
LA CITY HOUSING AUTHORITY
LA COLISEUM
LA FITNESS
LA FUEL CORPORATION
LA HARBOR DEPARTMENT
LA LOUVER
LA PARTNERSHIP
LA RECREATION & PARKS
LA ZIPPER
LAD INC AND
LAINER INVESTMENTS
LARRY BRENMAN
LARRY WONG
LAZBEN INVESTMENT INC.
LEO HEINRICH
LINCOLN ACADEMY VILLAGE
LINCOLN PROPERTIES
LONG DRUGS
LOS ANGELES AIRPORT-LAX
LOS ANGELES WORLD AIRPORT
LOYOLA MARYMOUNT UNIVERSITY
M & K PACIFIC REALTY
MAGDI GINDI
MANN THEATRES
MARC & JOANNE GEORGE
MARIE WIESL
MARKET PROPERTIES
MARLAND CO.
MASSOUD JAVADI
MAX ZIMBLER
MAY CENTER INC.
MAY DESIGN & CONSTRUCTION
MAY WAH INTERNATIONAL ENTERPRISE
MCMAHON/OLIPHANT-GLENDALE
MEDICENTER DEVELOPMENT INC.
MEHDIZADEH, DAVID
MEL ELLIOT
MERCURY AIR GROUP
MESMER PROPERTIES
METROPOLITAN WATER DISTRICT
MILLER, MILTON MR AND MRS
MITCHELL LITT
MONTY R. MOORMAN
MOTTA, TOM
MRS MURRELL
MTA
MULLIGAN LTD.
NATIONAL RAILROAD PASSENGER
NED YAMIN
NEW LOWE PROPERTIES
NIPPON CARGO AIRLINES
NIPPON MINIATURE BEARING CORP
NISSAN MOTOR CORPORATION (2)
NORTH HOLLYWOOD MED. PLAZA
NORTH VALLEY FAMILY YMCA
NORTHRIDGE HOLDING INC.
NORTHRIDGE IMAGING GROUP/DR
HOWARDBERGER
NUGGET CHEVROLET/KATY JEAN
ENTERPRISES
OFFICE DEPOT
OIL PROCESS CO.
ORANGE BANG/ DAVID FOX
P&R INVESTMENTS
PACIFIC BELL
PACIFIC RETAIL TRUST
PACIFIC YOUNGMAN DEV.
PAM MULLEN
PANORAMA TOWNE CENTER
PATRON'S AUTO CENTER
PEP BOYS
PEYKAR, GEORGE
PLAYA VISTA CAR CARE LTD.
PORT OF LONG BEACH
PORT OF LOS ANGELES
PORTER RANCH DEVELOPMENT
POUZANJANI, AMIR
PUBLIC STORAGE INC
PUENTE LEARNING CENTER
QANTAS AIRWAYS
QUEST FINANCIAL LLC
R T WOLFENDEN
R. EARL WELTY
RADFORD STUDIO CENTER INC.
RAHBAR
RALPH'S GROCERY CO.
RAYMOND BHATKA
RECTOR WARDENS AND VESTRY
RICHARD KICTIKOFF
RIKER LABORATORIES INC.
RITE AID CORPORATION
ROBERT RODRIGUEZ
ROCKWELL INTERNATIONAL
ROMERO
ROYAL-CLARK DEVELOPMENT
ROYAL-CLARK DEVELOPMENT
RUBY LEWIS
S & S ENTERPRISES
S R
SAMUEL A FRYER YAVNEH HEBREW
ACADEMY
SCHUBERT ORGAN (THEATRE)
SEACLIFF SEAFOODS
SEARS CO.
SELF-REALIZATION FELLOWSHIP
SHAPELL INDUSTRIES, INC.
SHIAU, CHIA TSO CO. TR
SHOW BIZ PIZZA TIME INC.
SILVER, BERNIE
SMART & FINAL
SMITH & HRICIK DEVELOPMENT
SMITH FOOD & DRUGS
SNYDER COMMERCIAL L.P
SOU PAC CO.
SPECTROLAB INC.
SPORTMART INC.
STAMFORD HOLDINGS NO. 2
STAPLES, INC.
STAR INVESTMENTS
STORAGE EQUITIES INC.
SUEN AND KYLA SHELGREN
SUNBELT INVESTMENTS
SUPER A FOOD INC.
SUPERIOR ELECTRIC
T-BIRD RESTAURANT
TAE HYUN KIM
TCW FOR TCW REALTY FUND
TEXACO REFINING & MARKETING
THE ARBA GROUP/WOODMAN & VA
THE YARMOUTH GROUP
THOMAS J. MCGARREY
TIME AVIATION SERVICES
TIMOTHY S. SULLIVAN
TOMMY TUCKER
TOQUAM PROPERTIES
TOSCO CORP.
TOYS R US
TRAVENOL LABORATORIES
TRI-UNION INTERNATIONAL LLC
TSAI-LIEN LIN
U-HAUL INTERNATIONAL
UNITED AIRLINES
UNIVERSAL CITY NISSAN
UNIVEST
USC PLANNING & CONSTRUCTION
VALLEY HOSPITAL MEDICAL CENTER
VALLEY KOREAN CENTER
VALLEY PRESBYTERIAN HOSPITAL
VALUE PRODUCE
VANOWEN INVESTMENT COMPANY
VAT PARTNERS
VENICE LTD
VENTURA CANOGA LTD PARTNERSHIP
VERA CAMPBELL
VLADMIR REIL
W AND S SHINBANE FAMILY LLC
WALL & PICO PARTNERSHIP
WARNER MARKETPLACE LLC
WELDON LTD. PARTNERSHIP
WEN CHEN
WILSHIRE BOULEVARD TEMPLE
WOODLAND HILLS COUNTRY CLUB
YASHIVA RAV ISACSOHN
YONGHOON CHO
YOUNG GENERATION VIDEO
YVETTE ACKERT

LIST OF ARTISTS

This index lists the many artists who have worked in the public art arena in Los Angeles either for Cultural Affairs, the Community Revelopment Agency, or the Metro Art Department, illustrating the scope of the art programs as well as the community of Los Angeles' artists. While the index lists an artist responsible for each work of art listed in this book, we want to acknowledge that each work of art is the result of a collaboration of many groups of people—the community participants; developers; City administrators; architects; contractors; teams of studio artists; fabricators—as well as artists.

KIM ABELES
JOSE ANTONIO AGUIRRE
LITA ALBUQUERQUE
LYNN ALDRICH
JACQUELINE ALEXANDER
TERRY ALLEN
ARMANDO ALVAREZ
MICHAEL AMESCUA
STEPHEN ANTONAKOS
JACKI APPLE
STEVE APPLETON
CHARLES ARNOLDI
WILLIAM ATTAWAY
ANDRO AVEDANO
JUDITH BACA
ROD BAER
GEORGE BAKER
PATRICK BAMBROUGH
MARY BARNES
MARLO BARTELS
HERBERT BAYER
JEAN-LUC BEGHIN
BILL BELL
BILLY AL
TONY BERLANT
RITA BLITT
JONATHAN BOROFSKY
RODGER BOYCE
MICHELE BOYER
ROBIN BRAILSFORD
TERRY BRAUNSTEIN
KATE BRAVERMAN
MARV BREHM
HORACE BRISTOL
DAVID BUNN
JOHN BUSCEMI
EUGENIA BUTLER
ALEXANDER CALDER
ED CARPENTER
SHELDON CARIS
CYNTHIA CARLSON
LEONORA CARRINGTON
GEORGE CASTANO
MARTHA CHATELAIN
CARL CHENG
ANNIE CHU
EVE COCKCROFT
WANDA COLEMAN
MEG CRANSTON
RIP CRONK
JOYCE DALLAL
MICHAEL DAVIS
WOODS DAVY
ALEJANDRO DE LA LOZA
DORA DE LARIOS
ALVIN T. DICKENS
CHARLES DICKSON
PAUL DIEZ
GUY DILL
LADDIE JOHN DILL
LINDSEY DION
MARK DI SUVERO
JESUS DOMINGUEZ
MARY LYNN DOMINQUEZ
JAMES DOOLIN
BETTY DORE
JACQUELINE DREAGER
JEAN DUBUFFET
RICARDO RODRIQUEZ
GARY DWYER
EAST LOS STREETSCAPERS
THOMAS EATHERTON
JUNE EDMONDS
RICHARD ELLIS
PETER ERSKINE
JOE FAY
BARBARA FIELD
KAY FINCH
JUD FINE
MICHAEL FLECHTNER
ELSA FLORES
STEVEN FREEDMAN
ELAINE FUESS
DIANE GAMBOA
ROSEMARY GARCIA
ELIZABETH GARRISON
LORENZO E. GHIGLIERI
ROBERTO GIL DE MONTES
DAVID GILHOOLY
DEAN GILLETE
BETTY GOLD
YOLANDA GONZALEZ
APRIL GREIMAN
GIDON GRAETZ
ROBERT GRAHAM
NANCY GRAVES
COLIN GRAY
TODD GRAY
MICHELLE GRIFFOUL
MINEKO GRIMMER
LAURIE GROSS
RAUL GUERRERO
MARK ERIC GULSRUD
CARL HAAG
RICHARD HALL
LLOYD HAMROL
JURICHIRO HANNYA
TIM HAWKINSON
MICHAEL HAYDEN
WAYNE HEALY
MILTON HEBALD
MICHAEL HEIZER
VICTOR HENDERSON
GEORGE HERMS
PAUL HERSHFIELD
MARU HOEBER
KRIS HOLLIDAY
BRAD HOWE
EUSTAQUIO INES
JIM ISERMANN
SENTARO IWAKI
GAN IWASHIRO
ROBERT JACOBS
JIM JENKINS
JOESAM.
TORGEN JOHNSON
JOHANNA JORDAN
WILLIAM JUDSON/JUDSON STUDIOS
WILLIAM JUDSON/JUDSON STUDIOS
DANIEL KEOHANE
SUE KIM
MARK KING
NANCY KINITSCH
JEROME KIRK
GEORGE KLEIMAN
SHEILA KLINE
KYONG SHIN KO
KAREN KOBLITZ
VITALY KOMAR
NOEL KORTEN
MICHIHIRO KOSUGE
MARK KOTANSKY
JOYCE KOZLOFF
B.J. KRIVANEK
NATALIE KROLL
SEIJI KUNISHIMA
CHO YIU KWAN
LILI LAKICH
SUSAN LANDAU
LIZ LARNER

LAURA LARSON
ANDREW LEICESTER
CHRISTOPHER LEE
MARK LERE
FRANCISCO LETELIER
ADAM LEVENTHAL
SHEILA LEVRANT DE BRETTEVILLE
PATTI LEWIS
JOE LEWIS
ALEXANDER LIBERMAN
LEO LIMON
PAO LING LIN
XAVIER LLONGUERAS
PETER LODATO
ALMA LOPEZ
KRISTINA LUCAS
GILBERT "MAGU" LUJAN
DEBRA MALSCHICK
CORK MARCHESCHI
DANIEL MARTINEZ
JACOB MARUISI
MICHAEL MASSENBERG
KAZUKO MATHEWS
PAUL MAXWELL
GALE MCCALL
BARBARA MCCARREN
VIQUI MCCASLIN
BLUE MCRIGHT
MICHAEL MEAKER
SERGIA MEIRON
ALEXANDER MELAMID
WILLIE MIDDLEBROOK
ROBERT MILLAR
MINEO MIZUNO
JOAN MIRO
PATRICK MOHR
MITZI MOGUL
ERNESTO R. MONTANO
DEBBIE MONTROSE
MANFRED MUELLER
MATT MULLICAN
GWYNN MURRILL
NOBUHO NAGASAWA
PATRICK NAGATANI
FRANK NARDINI
SUSAN NARDULI
BRUCE NAUMAN
MARGARET NEILSEN
WILLIAM NETTLESHIP
LOUISE NEVELSON
REIS NIEMI
MARGARET NIELSEN
ISAMU NOGUCHI
PATSY NORVELL
JOHN OKULICK
NONI OLABISI
CLAES OLDENBURG
ERIC ORR
ALBERTO OSSA
JOHN OUTTERBRIDGE
ANTHONY PARDINES
LOU PEARSON
RENE PETROPOULOS
DIANA PHILBROOK
ELLEN PHILLIPS
EMILE LOUIS PICAULT
JOE PINKELMAN
ELLIOTT PINKNEY
EDWIN PINSON
DAVID PLACHTE-ZUIEBACK
MICHELLE PLACHTE-ZUIEBACK
ANN PRESTON
ROBERT RAUSCHENBERG
ROBBIE ROBBINS
FRANK ROMERO
ERIKA ROTHENBERG
SANDRA ROWE
RICHARD ROWLEY
DAVID RUDOLPH
JAMES RUSSELL
BETYE SAAR
ROBERTO SALAS
CHRISTINA SCHLESINGER
KENNY SCHNEIDER
MICHAEL SCHOFIELD
TERRY SCHOONHOVEN
VICKI SCURI
JOHN A. (TONY) SHEETS
ERNEST SHELTON
SUSUMU SHINGU
PETER SHIRE
EDMOND E. SHUMPERT
ALEXIS SMITH
DON SMITH
WILLIAM SMITH
RUTH SNYDER
STARLIE SOKOL-HOHNE
STEVEN SORMAN
BUZZ SPECTOR
CHRISTOPHER SPROAT
DICK STARKWEATHER
THERMAN STATOM
JENNIFER STEINKAMP
FRANK STELLA
MARK STOCK
GEORGE STONE
OTTO 'TITO' STURCKE
EUGENE STURMAN
MARK SUMNER
MAY SUN
THOMAS SURIYA
JAMES SURLS
RODERICK SYKES
SHINKICHI TAJIRI
MICHAEL TANSEY
NEAL TAYLOR
RICHARD THOMAS
ROBERT TITTLE
MICHAEL TODD
SIMON TOPAROVSKY
ELOY TORREZ
JOHN TUCKER
RICHARD TURNER
KENT TWITCHELL
PAUL TZANETOPOULOS
DEWAIN VALENTINE
WALTER VALENTINE
PHILIP VAUGHN
COOSJE VAN BRUGGEN
DOUGLAS VAN HOWD
MATTHEW VANDERBORGH
DAVID VENEZKY
WARREN WAGNER
DEBRAH WARE
HORACE WASHINGTON
DARREN WATERSTON
SALLY WEBER
JOHN WEHRLE
RUTH WEISBERG
DONNA WEISNER
BILL WHEELER
DAUNA WHITEHEAD
SUSAN WICKSTRAND
DAVID WILKINS
STANELY WILSON
ADAM WOLPERT
RICHARD WYATT
KIM YASUDA
GEORGE YEPES
JODY ZELLEN
ELYN ZIMMERMAN

ACKNOWLEDGMENTS

Of course, this book could not have come to being without the work of the many artists, architects, fabricators, coordinators, sponsors and contributors. But in addition, we would like to thank those without whose research and advice this book could not have happened.

Aileen Farnan Antonier

Lesley Elwood

Maya Emsden

Felicia Filer

Cida Gonçalves

Mickey Gustin

Deborah Hart

Emily Hui

Mark Johnstone

Dennis Keeley

Jennifer Lin

Roella Hsieh Louie

Alexis Moore

Stefan Otto

Erik Qvale

Michael Several

Mo Shannan

Kendra Stanifer

THE EDITOR

Gloria Gerace most recently edited "The California Pop Up Book" for the Los Angeles County Museum of Art. She was executive producer of the film "Concert of Wills: Making the Getty Center" and the managing editor of "The Getty Center Design Process" and "Making Architecture: The Getty Center." She served as director of the exhibition "Making Architecture," and exhibition coordinator for The Hammer Museum's "The UnPrivate House."